American Work Trucks

A PICTORIAL HISTORY OF COMMERCIAL TRUCKS 1900-1994

D

Edited by John Gunnell

Published by

 krause
publications

700 E. State Street • Iola, WI 54990-0001
Telephone: 715/445-2214

Library of Congress Catalog Number: 93-80692
ISBN: 0-87341-290-7
Printed in the United States of America

Contents

Abbreviations

ACF	American Car & Foundry Company
CFR	crash/fire/rescue
CJ	Civilian Jeep
COE	cab over engine
DTM	Diamond T Motors
FWD	Four Wheel Drive Company
GMC	General Motors Corporation
GVW	gross vehicle weight
HD	heavy-duty
ICC	Interstate Commerce Commission
IHC	International Harvester Company
Indy	Indianapolis
Jr.	Junior
LCF	low cab forward
REA	Railway Express Agency
reefer	refrigerated truck
RPM	revolutions per minute
Rx	pharmaceutical
RV	recreational vehicle
SAE	Society of Automotive Engineers
UPS	United Parcel Service
US	United States
WP & L	Wisconsin Power & Light

Photo Credits

AA = Applegate & Applegate
AB = Art Bennett
AOS = A.O. Smith
ATC = Antique Truck Club
BAC = Brinks Armored Car
BP = Beetle Plastic
CMD = Chevrolet Motor Division
CN = Canadian News
CP = Crestline Publishing
CPI = Calendar Promotions, Inc.
CTC = Catepillar Tractor Company
DPL = Detroit Public Library
DTD = Dodge Truck Division
ECV = Encyclopedia of Commercial Vehicles
FMC = Ford Motor Company
FSU = Florida State University (Strozier Archives)
GTC = Goodyear Tire Company
GTR = General Tire & Rubber Company
HAC = Henry Austin Clark, Jr.
HUG = The Hug Company
IHC = International Harvestor Corporation
JA = James Allen
JAG = John A. Gunnell
JE = Joe Egle
JG = Jeff Gillis
JW = James A. Wren
KJC = Kaiser-Jeep Corporation
KTC = Kenworth Truck Company
LAB = Lawrence A. Brough

MHS = Minnesota Historical Society
MMC = Maxim Motor Company
MOC = M. O'Neil Company
MTI = Mack Truck, Incorporated
OAI = Outdoor Advertising Institute
OMD = Oldsmobile Motor Division
OMM = Old Motor Magazine
OTC = Oshkosh Truck Company
PFL = Philadelphia Free Library
PFZ = Peter F. Zierden
PTL = Passport Transport Limited
RG = Rick Gurid
RJG = Robert J. Gaylord
RK = Ron Kowalke
RPZ = R. Perry Zavitz
SPC = Studebaker Packard Corporation
TA = Texaco Archives
TST = The Seattle Times
TT = Truck Tracks
VAE = Vitralite Automobile Enamel
WFC = White Freightliner Company
WGM = Volvo GM Heavy Truck Corporation
WLB = William L. Bailey
WLF = Ward LaFrance
WMC = White Motor Corporation
WMT = Walter Motor Trucks
WSC = Warner & Swasey Company
WTC = Walter Truck Company
WTD = White Truck Division

Introduction

On a typical day, we awake to the sound (and the odor) of a fuel tanker making a delivery to the gas station next door. Soon we feel the rumble of the county highway crew's huge dump truck lumbering off to work in the wee hours. Minutes later, the wail of a siren and blast of an air horn are heard as a fire engine speeds by. Its shriek in the early dawn is answered by the hollow clanging and banging of wire racks in the Step-Van King delivering bread to the Quick-Stop next door. Then comes the "swish-boom" of the roll-up doors as the Pepsi routeman starts his early morning shift.

A utility van heading out to fix a downed wire; a farm truck with its stakes and racks squishing in huge piles of hay bales; a redi-mix truck bringing the road crew a "liquid" highway ... big trucks at work. That's what this book is about.

When we were kids, we all loved to watch trucks working at construction sites, on the docks, out in the fields or near a factory. Nothing compared to the sight of a titan cruising down the highway, pulling a 40-foot-long trailer behind it at 75 miles per hour. And it was absolutely amazing to watch that crane-truck lift those steel I-beams high in the air when the skyscraper was going up. Remember the airport crash/fire/rescue vehicles parked near that hangar when you flew to grandma's for Thanksgiving in 1963?

Now you have grown up. You have mouths to feed, bills to pay and deadlines to hit. Still, the little kid inside recalls the thrill of watching those brawny machines labor away. He remembers the bright colors, the gleaming chrome, the company logos on the side, the smoke billowing out of the exhaust stacks ... the sights ... the sounds ... the smells of American Work Trucks. That's what this book is about.

Today, people who love big trucks are finding and restoring them and collecting artifacts related to their history. The vehicles have names like Freightliner, Mack and Peterbilt, as well as Chevrolet, Dodge and Ford. The "truck-mobilia" that they collect ranges from license plates and log books to driver's badge caps and factory publicity photos.

American Work Trucks: A Pictorial History of Commercial Trucks 1900-1990 is a book that uses 600 such photos to trace the history of trucks and trucking from the earliest days to the current time.

The book begins with a series of essays about trucks, truck collecting and the trucking business. The essays were written by or about some of the leading personalities in the truck hobby, including Leigh Knudson, Larry Scheef, Elliott Kahn, Al Mroz, John Martin Smith, "Pop" Hays, Leon Schneper, Al Koenig, Alton O. Lust and Don Wood. It then showcases the hard-working commercial trucks of 10 decades in large-size photos with informative captions. These beautiful shots speak for themselves, providing a rich pictorial history of American Work Trucks.

Old Trucks are Fun!

By Leigh Knudson

This article is to serve as a warning to anyone considering getting involved with old trucks. As an illustration of what can happen, let me explain what has occurred since I first got involved in the truck hobby about 12 years ago.

Originally, all that I wanted was an early truck to restore. I didn't want a Ford or Chevrolet, since parts and restoration information for those marques were too readily available. I sought something more challenging. Eventually, I located a little 3/4-ton White in the San Francisco, California area. I bought it.

It didn't take long to realize that I had bought a lot bigger project than I realized. Advertisements for help, placed in car and truck collector magazines, brought little or no response. Finally, a lovely woman named Martha Ceder, of Cleveland, Ohio, read my plaintive ad. She responded. Martha was authorized to use the White Motor Company archives. She readily located a photo of my truck when it was new. That really got my restoration project moving.

The author got involved in the truck hobby after acquiring a 3/4-ton prewar White. This 1915 White calliope truck was a well-known attraction at Henry Austin Clark, Jr.'s Long Island Auto Museum. It is now owned by Wilfred Martkey Jr., Dallastown, Pennsylvania. (Henry Austin Clark, Jr. photo)

Letters to other White owners seldom generated any enthusiastic support for my project. However, I did locate a fellow named Roland O. Smith. He lived nearby and was also interested in early Whites, though he preferred those made after World War II. In 1985, Roland and I founded an organization for White truck owners. We called this group the Vintage White Truck Association (VWTA). We began publishing a magazine for the members on a twice a year basis.

Because of our White-related activities, we began to get noticed by some of the older and already established truck collectors and restorers. They encouraged our work and readily joined our newly formed organization. Volvo/GM Heavy Truck Corporation, the successor to White Motor Company, donated all their obsolete engineering drawings to VWTA. Currently, we have tens of thousands of these in our archives. We purchased a couple of file cabinets and filled them with White service manuals to answer technical inquires from VWTA members.

With VWTA established and work on our restorations progressing, we began to feel that chronic need that all restorers feel ... the need for obsolete components. Parts are needed whether they be NOS (new-old-stock), used, abused or just plain awful. The restorer is in constant need of new transfusion of parts.

To find parts, I began attending the Antique Automobile Club of America's (AACA) Fall National Meet in Hershey, Pennsylvania on a regular basis. Roland began going to Iola, Wisconsin's Iola Old Car Show most years. We both attended most of the local swap meets, too. Nevertheless, early White parts proved very scarce.

Our "inventory" grew. Originally, I needed parts for only one truck. Later, I bought another White to restore with my leftover parts. Then, I began collecting American truck emblems. In addition, Roland and I collected White sales literature from day one.

Since I liked visiting Hershey, the editor of the Antique Truck Club of America's Double Clutch offered me a deal. If I would write several articles for her magazine each year, I could stay at her house while attending the Hershey flea market a quarter of a mile away. Since I also attended the American Truck Historical Society's (ATHS) annual conventions, I realized I could combine my travel costs with a hobby business.

Undoubtedly one of the most stylish postwar trucks was the White 3000 COE. This 1951 version was used to deliver Coca-Cola. This basic model was built into the 1960s. (Applegate & Applegate photo)

I began buying, selling and trading truck lights. These included acetylene and kerosene lamps made specifically for trucks, as well as amber arrow style turn signals. This helped me to justify travel costs and allowed me to search for rare and unusual emblems, literature and early parts for my collections.

Of course, along the way, I bought a few more White trucks for parts. I have also acquired a few more interesting trucks to restore someday. In addition, I bought a couple of caches of early White NOS parts. In fact, I may have the best stock of White parts in the entire country.

Where has this all led? Roland and I spend most of our free time having a ball through our involvement with old trucks. We have both been president of our local Antique Truck HIstorical Society (ATHS) chapter. He is now national president of the largest truck club in the country, the American Truck Historical Society.

It seems like every weekend, we are off to a swap meet or wrecking yard. We get to travel all over the country and make friends by the hundreds. There are also many nice folks who we have never actually met, who call and write about their trucks and restoration problems. It is very unusual when a day passes that doesn't see one or two calls coming in about old trucks. Of course, my travel can be alternated with work on the growing inventory of truck lights or the restoration of actual trucks.

I have acquired a nifty bunch of early Whites. I have a large collection of truck emblems. I have a comprehensive White literature collection. But the most important thing is that the truck hobby has made my life richer and much more interesting. I literally know people all over the world as a result of my passion for old trucks.

Unless you want to get really involved with old trucks, steer clear of this hobby! Don't get started! Then, you won't have to drive across country delivering parts or visiting "truck nuts" or seeing your phone bills zoom like the national debt.

The one thing that makes truck collecting more fun than car collecting is that it's nearly classless. There are no ultra-expensive vehicles and it doesn't matter where your interests lie or what your social background is. Ex-presidents of major truck manufacturers will happily rub elbows with young, would-be mechanics since they both love the same thing and sing the same tune, "Old trucks are fun!"

(Leigh Knudson lives in Costa Mesa, California, where he collects emblems for all types of trucks, plus full-size White trucks and White Truck literature. When not working as a hobby dealer selling prewar White Truck parts and vintage commercial vehicle lights, he spends his time getting involved with ATCA, ATHS and AACA activities.)

Why Big Truck Collecting is Growing

By Larry L. Scheef

What makes the collecting and restoration of larger trucks of such an interest in the automotive hobby world of today?

The phenomenal new interest found in collecting large, antique trucks is partly brought on by that "little kid" inside us. Many Americans have always been fascinated by big, noisy trucks doing their work of the day. Be they fire trucks, black-smoke-bellowing highway rigs of the past, or mammoth construction trucks found at quarries and construction sites, they are fascinating.

I think we can all remember watching, with amazement while these monsters performed their tasks with what appeared to be minimal effort.

I think the memory of these behemoths awakens that child inside. Along with this, many collectors enjoy the new-found means to finance such an undertaking. Big trucks have perked the interest of many hobbyists. These are people who might otherwise collect small- to mid-sized trucks.

Families with construction backgrounds are restoring the trucks, like these 1930 Stewarts that were part of the nostalgia that made their companies what they are today. (Courtesy Peterbilt)

More such collectors are now getting into the challenge of restoring a large-sized truck. Many families with quarry or construction backgrounds have taken it upon themselves to restore a real part of the nostalgia that has made their company what it is today.

This nostalgia interest also holds true for many other related truck-using groups, such as house movers and heavy riggers. Collectors also include users of all kinds of fleet vehicles, from over-the-road highway tractors of the 1930s-1950s to the more specialized over-sized load "heavy haulers."

All of these groups find joy in showing the pride they have in their respective accomplishments. This is what makes the collecting and restoration of larger trucks of such an interest today.

(Larry L. Scheef is managing director of the American Truck Historical Society, an organization dedicated to the collection and preservation of the dynamic history of trucks, the trucking industry and its pioneers. He can be reached in care of ATHS, 300 Office Park Drive, Birmingham, Alabama 35223 or by calling (205) 870-0566.)

We can all remember watching, with amazement, while these monsters performed their tasks with what appeared to be minimal effort. This construction site was photographed on September 24, 1929. (Old Cars photo)

Collectors include users of all kinds of fleet vehicles including highway tractors of the 1930s. This 1938 Kenworth tractor even participated in the Great American Race. (Courtesy GreatRace Limited)

Trucks Spark Fascination and Plenty of Interest

By Elliott Kahn

I've been interested in things automotive all of my life, as far back as I can recall. I'm told it was even before then, that I could identify a passing car by the sound of its engine and transmission without actually seeing it. Automotive subject matter is immense and you never cease to learn new things about vehicles old and new.

A fascinating part of things automotive is the "truck." Our British friends call it the lorry. In Germany, it's the lastwagen. The Spanish term is camion. Even in America, the name has varied, over years, from carts, wagons and commercial cars to cartage carriers. Some folks describe them by their service use, such as a fire truck, a crane or a well-digger.

Many seem to think a vehicle is a truck only when it can cart a load of freight. In truth, a truck can be many things. For instance, a brand new truck chassis is often fitted with an aftermarket bus body. An old truck can be rebuilt and made into a bus at later time. In addition, a bus can be rebuilt as a truck, too. One of earliest vehicles the Mack Brothers built is now in a museum as a truck. It was originally a Manhattan brand bus.

Trucks come in all shapes and sizes. The number of wheels can vary. Some have just one axle, most have two, others have as many as 20. This is a 1916 "Bully" 3-wheel tractor with a conventional axle at the rear only. (Goodyear Tire & Rubber Company)

Although rated to carry one-ton loads, early trucks were often over-loaded. Some had two- or three-tons of stuff piled up and still made the trip. (State Photographic Archives, Strozier Library, FSU)

If you're a parts vendor, an old moving van might be nice for carting your things to flea markets or back home again. In addition, your family can sleep inside it. (Vitralite photo)

Big trucks are interesting, since they come in so many variations and can be equipped with thousands of bodies and paint jobs. This is 3-compartment tank body which was mounted on one of the 800 vehicles that Continental Oil Company of Denver, Colorado painted with Vitralite Automobile Enamel. (Vitralite photo)

13

Trucks are often service vehicles. They can take you to hospital in a hurry, or on your slow last ride to the cemetery. They can also cart you to war and bring you back home. They can change street lamp bulbs or paint a line down the center of the street. They can bring you a letter in the mail or a small packet by express service. They can haul off your garbage, carry your waste products, act as a workshop, service rolling shops, or function as a mobile hospitals or office. Those "big rigs" that haul trailers down the highway are combination homes and offices. The owner/operator and his family sometimes occupy the tractor's living quarters for weeks at a time. In a like manner, crews fighting fires or picking fruit may live in such units for a time.

Still another big use for trucks is in the construction industry. All types of construction vehicles are truck-based, including cranes, hoists and road surfacing vehicles. The same goes for trucks that haul concrete or do other such work. Some trucks are mining vehicles. Others may sweep your streets or do all sorts of chores.

The sizes of trucks can vary immensely. They can be miniature three-wheel machines with just a small platform on one end or side to carry tools, garbage or freight items. They can also be tremendously huge machines, such as the monstrous dump truck that carries 350 tons of rocks from a mine to a factory. There are huge, multi-axle units that can lift loads up to 700 tons to a construction site or in and out of a ship. Or how about a multi-unit machine with pieces that "plug" together and are operable by a single driver in one cab? These can actually consist of dozens of trucks, placed side-by-side or end-to-end, that move missiles or rockets onto launching pads. Some of these units carry thousands of pounds at one time. Some even carry thousands of tons!

It seems funny to hear people claiming the first American vehicle was not sold until late 1890s, since domestic trucks date back to 1886s or earlier. Most early trucks were fire apparatus. They include vehicles built to haul a pumper or tall ladder to the fire ground. Some early ones were steam-powered, while others were electric. A few made in the 1880s were powered by internal combustion engines. It's true that some of these had no steering. They were steered by horses or by a rail or track that they ran on. A few used a concrete or brick track to guide their wheels. Yet, they were self-propelled and moved along. The early Brown hoists, circa 1888, were huge machines that were usually steam or electrically operated. They could lift loads of 75 tons or more. And, yes, they did actually sell some of them.

Military trucks carry cannons, too, and machine guns used to make war on other trucks. This is a 1942 White half-track. (Courtesy General Tire Company)

14

Trucks come in all sizes. Some have just one axle, most have two, others have as many as 20. The one-axle jobs were designed to hook to a trailer or back segment to keep them from falling on the ground. To me, the big over-size trucks are among the most interesting, since they come in so many variations and can be equipped with thousands of bodies and paint jobs. In fact, in the 1970s, White Motors offered over 750 factory paint color combinations. Imagine how many trucks get custom paint jobs year after year! The number must range into hundreds of thousands. Trim can vary immensely with things like bright metal cabs, exhausts, fuel tanks, bumpers and mirrors, to works of graphic art and rolling paintings.

A truck can be beautiful, but it can also be hideous-looking. No matter which is the case, all trucks are interesting. For a small child (like me) in the 1920s, even a relatively small Model TT Ford truck was huge, compared to the size of person. Although rated to carry just a one-ton load, the Ford trucks were usually over-loaded. Some had two- or three-tons of stuff piled up and still usually made the trip.

Today, most trucks with such loads are bigger, but the interest and variety is still there. You can watch as the circus arrives and see some very interesting vehicles. First, there's the animal cages on wheels. Then comes the carnival crew, setting up its wares and using certain trucks as a base for amusement park rides. On some circus trucks, you will see the cannons that shoot clowns into the air.

Military trucks carry cannons, too, and machine guns used to make war on other trucks. Para-military vehicles include police vans and paddy wagons to take crooks to the "pokey." Mobile holding cells and portable jails are also used in some areas today.

Today, most of us depend on things brought by highway trucks. However, some trucks ride on tracks, on skis, or on rails. Many years ago in Colorado, a Pierce-Arrow car was converted to a bus/truck and used by railroad track maintenance crews. Today, we have trucks that can roll along a highway and then be converted to run on rails. This is accomplished by lowering a flanged set of wheels to substitute for the rubber tires.

In Spanish-speaking countries the term for truck is camion. This camion ran off the road in Costa Rica and caused a traffic tie-up. (Darryl Glen Cole photo)

15

Trucks are certainly impressive. A 240-ton dump truck that holds your house in its box might be too large for most collectors, but there are many commercial vehicles of all ages to find. Look for one that holds your interest or stirs up questions or relates to something you want to learn about. An old ice truck might be just the right thing for you. Or maybe you prefer a Zamboni that can scrape the ice or absorb moisture off a wet field?

Most trucks were built for a purpose. Find the one that best suits your needs. If you're an auctioneer, you might want a big, flat platform-bodied truck. You can stand above the crowd, on the platform, looking good and conducting your business. If you're a parts vendor, an old moving van might be nice for carting your things to flea markets or back home again. In addition, your family can sleep inside it. Or how about the vehicle that loans books? (a traveling library); does your laundry? (a rolling laundromat); or cleans your shop? There are also rolling stores for lawn care items; pet care; hair cutting; and cleaning services.

The materials trucks are made of can also vary immensely. They have been built of plastic, wood, all kinds of metals, pressed paper and even pressed sawdust.

I recall when custom-bodied cars were of interest to me. They are valuable and collectible because they're rare. But custom trucks? Just go out on the highway, visit a nearby truck stop, or drop in at a truck dealer. What you will see might amaze you. Custom trucks range from a church (with a chapel for services in the back of the tractor) to a food vending model that can make you a sandwich, a dessert or a multi-course dinner. It not only cooks the food, but packages it for you.

Auto history buffs may find it fascinating to learn that most car builders have made trucks at one time or another. In fact, Henry Ford was chief engineer for the old Detroit brand of truck made from the late 1890s to about 1901. Another pioneer automaker, Ransom E. Olds, also built early trucks and buses. One of his earliest models was a 1901 Curved Dash Olds with a parcel carrier on back. Olds also built two big electric trucks between 1899 and 1901. One carried a 3-ton load and the other was rated at 5-tons. Oldsmobile offered trucks for some years, as did Mr. Olds' later firm, Reo.

Whatever your hobby goals and interests are, don't overlook big trucks as worthwhile collectibles. As we indicated at the start, antique trucks can be fascinating and spark immense enthusiasm. They are certainly as much fun as old cars, but they offer a much larger variety of options, custom equipment and special-purpose equipment to make them unique and endearing.

(Elliott Kahn is a veteran automotive historian whose truck research credits include contributions to The Encyclopedia of Commercial Vehicles, Wheels of Time, and other publications. When not enjoying automotive writing and photography, he spends his time enjoying the warm Florida sun.)

All types of construction vehicles are truck-based, including cranes, hoists and road surfacing vehicles. This is a 1979 Oshkosh tractor hauling a crane on a heavy-duty low-boy trailer. (Oshkosh Truck Company)

The A.W. Hays Truck Museum

By Albert Mroz

Just outside the Sacramento (California) Airport stands one of the largest vintage truck collections in the United States, containing 192 trucks representing 129 different manufacturers.

The A.W. Hays Truck Museum was built by A.W. "Pop" Hays and his family. Hays collected trucks for 20 years after his retirement from the trucking business. He died in November 1992 at the age of 91.

Hays spent all his life involved with trucks. In Burney, California, where he was born, he began driving and repairing trucks at age 16. He was 17 when World War I ended and, by the time he was 28, he had his own trucking company: A.W. Hays Trucking Incorporated.

Hays started in 1929, at the outset of the depression. "With my entire savings of $250, I put a down payment on a new 1929 Chevrolet 1-1/2-ton truck," Hays said in August 1992. "That's when I really got started."

This 1916 Garford 2-ton gas tanker truck greets thousands of visitors to the A.W. Hays Truck Museum. It was also featured on cable television's "Truckin' U.S.A." program. (A. Mroz photo)

17

Very important folks at the A.W. Hays Museum include (left to right) technical curators Homer Kerr and Nord Johnson, founder A.W. "Pop" Hays and director Don Hays. (A. Mroz photo)

On a business challenge from a farmer, Hays began hauling live poultry from Corning to San Francisco. He drove at night, to prevent the chickens' exposure to heat and sun, which would often kill half of them en route. Hays was nearly 100 percent successful with his method and got the contract.

"No, I didn't make the chickens fly to ease the load," Hays joked last year. "I worked 60 hour weeks hauling products in the central valley."

Trucks represented in the museum read like a who's who of American manufacturing: from Acme, Aetna, Alco and All American to Wilcox, Winther, Wolverine and Yellow-Knight. This is the 1919 Parker 3-1/2-ton. (A. Mroz photo)

Over the years "Pop" Hays built the business into the largest agricultural carrier in California. Hays was the originator of the hopper trailer and was one of the first to use a two-way radio in trucking in 1959. When he sold his business in 1977, the first thing he wanted to do was to find his original 1929 Chevrolet truck. It wasn't around anymore, but another one just like it has been restored and is on display in the museum.

Visitors delight in seeing rare vehicles not found elsewhere, such as the 1901 Knox with its one-cylinder "porcupine" air-cooled engine. The 1909 Sears brings to mind the days when Sears had everything in its catalog, including cars, trucks and prefabricated homes. The 1916 Commercial Truck Electric was used by the Curtis Publishing Company in its 22-vehicle fleet as late as 1962. It and a 1918 Walker Electric Truck bring to mind recent legislation that will put electric vehicles on the roads again.

Many trucks, such as the 1922 MacDonald, 1927 Fageol and 1930 Dodge are from an era when trucks were built in Northern California. Before the depression, there were truck manufacturers in practically every region of the country. Companies such as Graham, Maxwell, Nash, Oldsmobile, Packard, Pierce-Arrow, Reo

The Hays Museum's 1921 Defiance motor truck. (A. Mroz photo)

and Studebaker are familiar names as classic cars, but they also built trucks at one time.

As visitors from all over the world enter the museum, a 1937 1-1/2-ton Diamond T tanker gleams with the aerodynamic form of mid-1930s art deco design. Exemplifying the early "Bubble nose" aluminum-body COE designs pioneered by Freightliner in Portland, Oregon, a 1949 Model 800 truck tractor is one of the 56 original units built. The newest truck presently in the collection is a 1956 White. Out of the 129 different manufacturers represented, only a dozen are in business under the same name today.

One of the biggest differences between a museum of classic cars and one full of old trucks is that the old trucks were never pampered, like most of the exotic or expensive cars undoubtedly were. Some of the trucks in the museum have been restored from rusty derelicts to proud original condition by curator Nordstrom Johnson and museum volunteers. But, just as many of the trucks are preserved in average street condition, reminding us of the beating these vehicles endured during their life of utility and transport. The rough life explains why some of these trucks are, in many instances, singular examples from their production runs long ago. These vehicles either did their job or they joined the scrap heap.

Few, if any, were kept for their aesthetic value. Now, though, looking back nearly a century, we can see the many trends, inventions, innovations and smart details employed in their manufacture. As there were once numerous contenders in the truck building industry, the trucks represented in the museum read like a who's who of American manufacturing: from Acme, Aetna, Alco and All American to Wilcox, Winther, Wolverine and Yellow-Knight.

The A.W. Hays Truck Museum is located at 2000 East Main Street, Woodland, California 95695, on the corner of Route 102 just off Interstate 5. Hours are 9 a.m. to 3 p.m. every day. Admission is $3 for adults and $1 for children 6 to 12. Telephone number is (916) 661-1167.

(Don Hays, director of the A.W. Hays Truck Museum, selected this article by Albert Mroz for its brief, but accurate portrayal of the museum's history and contents. Albert Mroz has also had his work published in The San Francisco Examiner, AutoWeek, Go West, Pickup and Delivery, Nevada City Union and elsewhere. He has received the Phelan Literary Award.)

Down in the "Dumps" Since 1928

By Alton O. Lust

My life has been involved with dump trucks since 1928. I started my trucking career that year behind the wheel of a 1925 Model T Ford dump truck that I drove for A.T. Riese Trucking Company of Brodhead, Wisconsin. The truck had no cab. Its commercial equipment consisted mainly of a windshield, an old seat on the gas tank and a homemade 1-yard gravity dump body.

We were hauling crushed rock with the Model T for a highway project near Mt. Vernon, Wisconsin. When we finished it, I got a job with H.H. Thousand Trucking Company of Mt. Horeb. It required driving a 2-1/2-yard Stoughton truck with a mechanical lift body. That was a step up from the Model T!

The next year I took employment with John Beale of Madison. This involved driving a new Reo Speedwagon truck equipped with a Heil hoist and a 3-yard dump body. I drove this truck until August 21, 1930, when I purchased a new Model A Ford truck equipped with a 2-yard Heil body and an hydraulic hoist.

In the fall of 1931, I traded the Ford for a new 1931 International (IHC) Model A4 with a 3-yard dump body and Heil hydraulic hoist. This truck was used to haul crushed rock in the summer and to plow winter snow. I sold it in the fall of 1933.

This 1927 Chevrolet dump truck was one of 50 vehicles that the Walrath-Sherwood Company of Omaha, Nebraska, painted with Vitralite Automobile Enamel. Note the lift mechanism ahead of rear wheel. (Vitralite)

With WPA projects supplementing private construction during the depression, some owners of dump truck fleets enjoyed growth. This fleet of nine 1932 Mack dump trucks was built by National Steel Products Company. (Joe Egle)

In the fall of 1931, Alton O. Lust purchased a new 1931 IHC 3-yard dump body. This photo shows a row of IHC trucks of the same era with dump bodies built by National Steel Products Company. (Joe Egle)

On August 21, 1930, Lust purchased a new 1931 Model A Ford truck equipped with a dump body. It was somewhat similar to this truck restored by Masche Trucking of Lake Mills, Wisconsin. (Old Cars photo)

A used 1928 Model 54 IHC with a Heil 4-yard dump body and hydraulic hoist was purchased in the spring of 1934. Later, it was sold to a house mover in Cuba City. I then bought a used Ford with a 2-1/2-yard Heil body and it hauled "Ag-lime" to farmers for a Works Project Administration (WPA) program. The job proved big enough to purchase a 1930 Chevrolet with a dump body.

In the spring of 1935, I traded my two old trucks for a used Ford V-8 model. It had a 3-yard Heil hydraulic dump body. Late the same year, I obtained a used 1934 Ford V-8 with a similar body and used both trucks on a big highway project for P.W. Ryan of Janesville. The next year, a used 1935 Ford with a Heil 4-yard hydraulic dump body joined the fleet. We worked for the WPA building Madison's airport.

This pretty dump truck is a rare Indiana Six of about 1930 vintage. It was operated by the Stewart Sand Material Company. The body was built by National Steel Products Company. (Joe Egle)

This fleet of dump trucks, believed to be constructed on 1927 White chassis, may have totaled 26 vehicles, judging from the way the trucks are identified on their tailgates. They are not in alphabetical order, though. (Joe Egle)

The four truck level was reached in the spring of 1937, when I bought a new Ford V-8 with a Heil 4-yard dump body. That same fall, I got a used 1934 Model B4 International. It was used to plow snow during 1937 and 1938. Then, we put a dump box on it and hauled crush rocks for other projects in Dane County. We also worked near Elizabethville, Illinois for Hanson & Jackson, who were contractors from Blanchardville, Wisconsin. Several more jobs with them followed in 1937, 1938, 1939 and 1940.

In 1940, the old International was traded for a new Model D35 IHC truck equipped with a Heil dump body and an hydraulic hoist. This unit brought my fleet up to five trucks. We were growing again! We had hauling contracts with Evenson Contractors of Cambridge, Norm Carpenter of Rockdale and Drew & Gary of Evansville (Wisconsin) during 1941. That fall, I bought a 1942 Ford chassis. The dump box from one of the 1935 Fords was transplanted to the chassis and the old cab and chassis was retired.

Art Overgard contracted with us to haul crushed stone for a project in western Dane County in the spring of 1942. When this was done, it was off to Camp McCoy, where we did work for P.W. Ryan once again. This involved building roads and streets at the army base. We stayed there until the fall of 1944, when Camp McCoy was finished.

After the early years, my company continued contract hauling for several contractors and enjoyed consistent growth. Eventually, I wound up with a fleet of 44 dump trucks. Most were

A 1927 White with a wood "grain box" dump body and a hoist manufactured by National Steel Products Company of Kansas City, Missouri. (Joe Egle)

Here is the 1927 White with the dump box up. The hoist is designed to swing to the sides so the box can be raised and lowered. (Joe Egle)

Fords and IHCs. I retired in 1985, after 55 years in the business. All of my trucks were sold off to different people.

After retirement, I found that I still had trucking in my blood. I have kept busy restoring a 1930 IHC Model A4 and a 1933 Ford pickup, plus three old cars.

(Alton O. Lust of Mt. Horeb, Wisconsin operated Alton O. Lust Construction Hauling Company for 55 years. He has been involved with dump trucks since 1928 and was a member of the Wisconsin Road Builders Association. On May 28, 1993, at the American Truck Historical Society convention in Milwaukee, he was presented with a Founder's Award.)

Truck Memorabilia Collecting Explodes

By Allen I. Koenig

Interest in old trucks and trucking history has exploded in recent years. The growth of ATHS (American Truck Historical Society) has mirrored this interest. Recently, net membership appears to be growing in the area of 1,000 members every six to eight months. Although it would appear that interest in all facets of transportation, air and rail included, is at a high level, only within the past decade has interest in the history of trucking really began to increase.

Not everyone in the old truck category is interested in restoring old vehicles, however. It appears that the collecting of models, photographs, route guides, trade magazines and other memorabilia of all kinds is red hot. All of these areas of interest harken back to the "good old days" indeed. Puny gas power, inadequate heaters and defrosters, vacuum brakes, tiny mirrors, dim lights and tough seats were the benchmark of those days ... the 1930s, 1940s and 1950s.

Early truck drivers were real "Dapper Dan's" with their caps, collars and neckties. (Goodyear Tire & Rubber Company)

Jack Mitchell was named California State Driver of the Year in 1969. The Pacific Intermountain Express (PIE) driver is seen here with Miss U.S.A. and Miss Chinatown U.S.A. 1969. (Photo courtesy of Al Koenig)

His hat badge identifies this well-dressed truck driver as a proud employee of Nickles' Bakery Company. His uniform and necktie make him look almost as neat as his 1957 Studebaker 3E11 standup delivery van. (Applegate & Applegate)

We are fortunate to find many of those industry pioneers alive today; people who can paint a clear picture of the glory years trucking. ATHS has formally been recognizing those hundreds of pioneers who built highway transportation into the keystone of our great industrialized society here in America.

I would like to briefly describe one area of collecting which typifies a growing sector of trucking collectibles: the history of the drivers' hat badges.

Just as the wrist watch replaced the pocket watch in the 1920s, the wardrobe of the well-dressed truck driver of the 1960s changed from uniforms, ties, hats and badges to baseball caps and leisure clothing. Gone were the days of the uniformed driver with a necktie and all the trimmings that symbolized a very proud era of the motor carrier industry during the 1930s to 1950s.

"Pledged to Courtesy and Safety: ATA" patches and decals decorated the uniforms and truck doors of many fleets. Driver's hats were adorned with numerous safe driving awards from the American Trucking Association, insurance companies and Markel. A leader in this movement, Gene Johnson, executive vice president of Pacific Intermountain Express (PIE), conceived the P-I-E image program. It was patterned after airline industry programs, complete with full color coded uniforms, shirts, ties and hats.

Hand-in-glove with this successful program was P-I-E's "Good Citizen of the Highways" image program. Johnson's ideas led the industry in an overall image upgrade. It depicted genuine concern in sharing the highways with other motorists and rewarded drivers for deeds of courtesy and accident prevention. Behind this concept was a plan to portray the fledgling trucking industry as a "bankable" industry that was acceptable to bankers, lenders and insurers.

Prior to this era, trucking was considered a very risky business. Johnson wanted to change that perception. Many other trucking companies followed his idea, which was a very positive concept indeed.

An important part of the professional image program was to distinctly identify the drivers and companies from each other. Embroidery, as it is known today, was not readily available. To fill the need, metal and enamel hat badges became popular.

One of the pioneers in the hat badge business was Manuel Gorriaran, who founded Hook-Fast Buckle Company in 1922. Later, he complemented his line of buckles and belts with tie clasps, badges, nameplates and money clips. During the 1940s and 1950s, Hook-Fast marketed badges through truck stops and independent salesmen. It also designed custom logo badges for many trucking companies. Today, Hook-Fast continues as a supplier to the police, airline, taxi, bus and fire fighting segment of the economy.

Most companies that manufactured hat-badges for truckers originated as suppliers of emblems for fire fighters and law enforcement personnel, such as these California Highway Patrol officers. (Richard Kelley photo collection)

It was over 100 years ago that the Bastian Brothers began their emblematic manufacturing business. They provided badges and emblems for police personnel and fire fighters and later supplied products for vehicle manufacturers such as Ford, General Motors and Kenworth, as well as hat badges for trucking companies. Construction machinery watch fob collectors will also recognize Bastian as a premier watch fob creator.

Other badge companies evolved, too. They included Salt Lake Stamp Works, Northwestern Stamp Works, St. Paul Stamp, Sach-Lawlor and Entensmann.

My own involvement in badges evolved over the years, due to an interest in trucks, art and jewelry. Today, many trucking company badges can correctly be considered as excellent examples of art deco items. The many individual designs and the use of cloissine enamels have insured their collectability today. Although thousands were created, pristine examples are extremely-difficult to acquire. Many are in collections, both large and small. Unknown numbers are hidden in attic boxes, dresser drawers and garage corners. Most likely, many are resting in landfills and dumps, never to be admired again.

To serious collectors, including this writer, the search will continue.

(Alan I. Koenig is president of Midwest Specialized Transportation, Incorporated of Rochester, Minnesota. He is a well-known Kenworth collector and serves as the chairman-of-the-board for the American Truck Historical Society.)

The uniformed trucker with necktie and trimmings symbolized a proud era of the motor carrier industry in the 1930s to 1950s. This Great Southern Trucking Company driver steers a 1936 Ford tractor. (Applegate & Applegate photo)

Pioneer Antique Truck Collector and Restorer

By Kerry Day

"Mr. Trux" is the nickname folks have bestowed on Leon Schneper of New Vernon, New Jersey. He earned it by being one of the pioneer collectors and restorers of antique trucks in the northeast.

Leon Schneper's love of trucks began, at an early age, when his father bought a 1919 Diamond T truck to use on the family's farm. By the spring of 1920, nine-year-old Leon was driving it on the farm. At the age of 12, he was stopped by the local police for driving without a license.

His experience with trucks continued as a driver. At a young age, he signed on to work for many local companies. One used a chain-drive Mack "Bulldog" that worked transporting tar for road building.

"Mr. Trux" sits in his favorite spot, behind the steering wheel of the 1927 Mack AC "Bulldog" tractor that he restored. (Michael A. Carbonella photo)

Parked near his home in New Vernon, New Jersey is Leon Schneper's 1914 Autocar two-cylinder delivery wagon. (Michael A. Carbonella photo)

Schneper's involvement with trucks and his construction-related activities led him to start his own contracting and sand and gravel business in 1946. After running it successfully for many years, Schneper retired in 1967. He has been active in the restoration of antique trucks ever since.

Surprisingly, Schneper's first vehicle restoration involved a car. The 1905 Cadillac roadster was completed in 1954. That experience, and his fondness of old trucks, motivated him to restore an old truck in 1958. He was also inspired by the fact that the Antique Automobile Club of America (AACA), which he belonged to, had just created a commercial vehicle classification.

The first truck restored by Leon Schneper was his 1919 White Model 15, which has appeared in commercials, motion pictures and other books. (Michael A. Carbonella photo)

29

Leon's early years in his new hobby were unique, as truck collecting was teething in the late-1950s and early 1960s. Not too many people were involved with restoring trucks back then. In fact, trucks were rarely thought of as collectibles. After serving their owners well for many years, they were simply "put out to pasture" when worn out. That's exactly where Schneper found his 1919 White Model 15 flatbed truck in 1958.

This truck was discovered in a pasture in Deans, New Jersey. It was in rough shape, having endured many cold winters outside. Schneper spent three years completely restoring the White to mint condition. His skill and craftsmanship resulted in an AACA national first place award. This truck went on to become very famous as the star of television commercials for Breakstone's Cottage Cheese, Plymouth brand chicken and Sperry Rand products. To add to the truck's credits, it appeared in the motion pictures "The Great Gatsby" and "Godfather: Part II," as well as in the color section of The Complete Encyclopedia of Commercial Vehicles.

Leon Schneper and his White became very well known and, without a doubt, helped promote the antique truck hobby in its formative stages. He did not stop with the White, though. Schneper spent many hours combing the countryside looking for more old trucks and parts for them. Driving the back roads of New Jersey, New York and Pennsylvania, Schneper searched for old trucks in back yards, open fields and salvage yards.

In 1971, Schneper's dedication to the hobby led to his involvement as one of the re-organizers of the Antique Truck Club of America (ATCA). This experience exposed him to many more opportunities to find, buy and restore other antique trucks. The growing fraternity of restorers and collectors benefited, too, from Leon's devotion to his hobby. He helped many individuals find parts or suggested where they could find a specialist to fix their old trucks. The ATCA has honored him with the "Leon Schneper Trucker's Choice Trophy," presented at their annual truck show in Macungie, Pennsylvania.

In 1983, as a member of the American Truck Historical Society (ATHS), Leon Schneper helped start the organization's Metro Jersey chapter as a charter member. Here again, he helped many members with various projects and in supporting the new group morally and financially.

Leon Schneper's restoration of the first of his three 1930 Mack BL trucks, with the help of Tom Spencer, resulted in a beautiful stake bed example of this model being preserved. It may be the only one in the country. (Kerry Day photo)

Over the past 36 years, Schneper has bought, sold and collected more than 30 antique trucks. The most notable examples that he has owned or helped bring back to life are: 1919 White Model 15 flatbed; 1914 Autocar two-cylinder delivery wagon; 1927 Mack AC tractor and heavy equipment trailer; 1948 Mack LJ tractor; 1914 Diamond T delivery; 1918 Mack AC dump truck; 1930 Mack AC tractor with Cummins four-cylinder diesel; 1928 Mack AB flatbed; and 1948 Mack EG. Today, many of these vehicles are part of collections maintained by other truck lovers throughout the country. Schneper does not have the room to store all of these relics of the past.

Dot Schneper, Leon's wife of 56 years, is convinced that his hobby has kept him young of heart and mind. After receiving a pacemaker last year, Schneper was able to continue his pursuit of unique antique trucks. In fact, he is now in the second year of his latest, and perhaps most challenging, restoration project.

Schneper's new project revolves around three 1930s vintage Mack BL trucks, two of which were purchased from a collection in Wilkes Barre, Pennsylvania. They were in rough shape, with wrecked cabs and frozen motors. The fact that these Macks are fairly rare and that, apparently, no restored examples survive in the United States, seemed all the more reason for Leon to take up the challenge. A restoration of the first of the three trucks, with the help of Tom Spencer (a Warren, New Jersey restorer), resulted in a beautiful example of this model being preserved.

Schneper readily admits that the restoration of rare old trucks can get expensive. The Mack project was no exception. "Restoring the radiator shell for just one truck cost more than my initial purchase of all three trucks," Mr. Trux reported. However, the recent completion of the job also brought him much pleasure and enjoyment.

Schneper gets a lot of pleasure from driving his old trucks. Operating the ancient vehicles is fun. Though sometimes quite challenging to drive, the old trucks are real attention-getters.

Back in 1962, soon after the 1919 White was restored, Leon and Dot drove it from New Jersey to Niagara Falls, New York. The trip proved to be an adventure complete with mechanical failures and a flat tire. However, it did prove to be a personal triumph seeing the old White cover so many miles some 42 years after it was first built.

Another experience that he had on the road always gives Schneper a chuckle. It seems that a trucker in a modern rig pulled up alongside him, while he was driving his 1927 Mack AC tractor, pulling a trailer loaded with the 1919 White and the 1914 Autocar. The trucker stared in disbelief and said, "What happened? Did they stick you with the old one today?"

Despite his 82 years, Leon Schneper is always ready to drive anyone's antique truck nearly anytime or anywhere. He says he's not sure how many more projects he'll be able to start and finish, but hints that he'd like to restore a second of the three Mack BLs.

Those who have met Leon Schneper can probably agree that he's likely to achieve that goal ... as well as many others. Mr. Trux thrives on his favorite hobby and seems always ready to meet the challenge at hand.

If you are driving the roads of northern New Jersey, keep a sharp lookout for an old Mack traveling the byways. You may well spot Leon Schneper behind the wheel, enjoying himself while simply touring or traveling to his next antique truck show.

(Kerry Day is a member of the American Truck Historical Society's Metro New Jersey Chapter which was chartered, with the help of Leon Schneper, in 1983.)

Trucks Big and Little a Big Part of New Museum

By John Martin Smith

The National Automotive and Truck Museum of the United States (NATMUS) will preserve and interpret the history of trucks and trucking. Established in 1991, NATMUS is located in the former factory buildings of the Auburn Automobile Company, in Auburn, Indiana. It sits near the intersection of I-80/90 and I-69 in the heartland of America.

Trucks have been the lifeblood flowing through the arteries of the American economic system for nearly a hundred years, but they have been largely neglected in history books and in museums. NATMUS has been very well received by truck collectors and historians and by the general public. The NATMUS buildings contain over 100,000 square feet of display space and are located on 5.25 acres of land. This large complex will enable NATMUS to preserve and interpret the industry through a mixture of vehicles and memorabilia. Displays already include period vehicles, signs, books and literature, plus a circa 1948 Valentine Diner.

A museum within a museum, the National Automotive and Truck Model and Toy Museum (NATMATMUS) collects and preserves model and toy cars and trucks. These will be displayed and interpreted, along with their full-sized counterparts. Several model and toy companies have already named NATMATMUS as their archive for each item which they manufacture.

A museum within a museum, the National Automotive and Truck Model and Toy Museum collects and preserves model and toy cars and trucks, including antiques similar to these Keystone and Buddy L items. (Old Cars photo)

To support research, the National Automotive and Truck Library of the United States (NATLUS) has been made a part of NATMUS. It contains books and literature pertaining to the history of the industry.

NATMUS/NATMATMUS is located adjacent to the Auburn-Cord-Duesenberg Museum, which houses a prestige collection of classic and Indiana built cars.

NATMUS is supported by memberships, admissions and the donations of individuals, corporations and trusts and foundations. Donations of vehicles, toys and models, and books and literature are also sought by the 501 (c)(3) not-for-profit museum institution. Donations are deductible to the extent of their present fair market value, regardless of their cost or basis.

A brochure containing membership and donation information is available by calling (219) 925-4560, faxing (219) 925-4563 or writing NATMUS/NATMATMUS, Box 686, Auburn, IN 46706.

(John Martin Smith practices law in Auburn, Indiana. He has long been a "spark plug" behind the success of the city's ACD Museum and its many classic car activities. He became president of NATMUS-NATMATMUS after it was established two years ago.)

Toy trucks will be displayed and interpreted at NATMATMUS. The Smith-Miller Bekins van and other toys shown are from a private collection, but represent types that NATMATMUS would like to acquire through donations. (Old Cars photo)

Several model and toy makers have named NATMATMUS as their archive for each item they manufacture. This Ertl model, honoring the 20th anniversary Iola Car Show, is representative of toys welcome in the archives. (Iola Car Show photo)

Teamsters!

By Donald F. Wood
Professor of Transportation
San Francisco State University

Teamsters deserve their share of credit for the development of trucking during the 20th Century. They evolved from being drivers of local drayage wagons that were pulled by teams of horses, hence their name. Local delivery operations were slowly motorized with either gas or electric trucks; although the writer recalls seeing horse-drawn rigs in the Boston Produce Market as late as 1960.

Teamsters evolved as drivers of drayage wagons pulled by teams of horses, hence their name. Local delivery operations were slowly motorized with either gas or electric trucks like this 1918 Federal. (Dale Thompson photo)

34

In the 1920s, trucks began over-the-road service between cities. The drivers kept the "teamster" name. Trucking developed fully in the 1930s as paved highways linked most major cities so this 1935 Federal could roll. (Old Cars)

Warehousemen and driver helpers, like those unloading this 1954 Diamond T delivery van, were covered by lucrative contracts the Teamsters union won for its members. (Applegate & Applegate photo)

Teamster unionization was important to the labor movement because union drivers refused to cross picket lines set up by their brother union members. This teamster drove a 1956 Diamond T with an Andrews trailer. (Old Cars)

In the 1920s, trucks began performing over-the-road service between cities and their drivers kept the "teamster" name. The industry developed fully in the 1930s, as paved highways connected all major cities. The teamster was expected to make his own repairs and change tires along the way. Teamsters also began unionizing. This was important to the labor movement as a whole, because unionized drivers would refuse to cross picket lines established by their brother union members.

At the same time some drivers saw their protection within unions, others became small scale capitalists. These entrepreneurs became known as owner-operators. They owned their own rigs (although often in conjunction with one or more finance companies) and hired themselves out on a load-by-load basis. Often, they were badly exploited.

After World War II, trucking continued its explosive growth and the Teamsters union gained national power. The International Brotherhood of Teamsters, Chauffeurs, Warehousemen and Helpers of America was able to win many lucrative contracts for its members. These contracts did not hobble the trucking industry in the manner that rail unions were hobbling the railroads. Teamster leaders also developed ties with organized crime and, for a time, became an embarrassment to the rest of the organized labor movement.

Trucking deregulation, which took place in 1980, was a successful effort at reducing the Teamsters' power.

Despite the public's disapproval of Teamster leaders, the individual truck driver continues to be a folk hero and is, to many, the 20th Century cowboy. Rugged, independent, and lonely, the drivers are in our thoughts whenever we meet them on the road, pause at a truck stop or hear a forlorn Country and Western ballad.

(Donald F. Wood is a Professor of Transportation in the School of Business at San Francisco State University. He co-authored several college text books and serves as a consultant to numerous public and private agencies. Don writes about old trucks as a hobby. His credits include the books Chevy El Camino 1959-1982 Photofacts and American Volunteer Fire Trucks. He is also a contributor to the Standard Catalog of American Light-Duty Trucks.)

Trucks go to Hershey, too

By John A. Gunnell

The Antique Automobile Club of America (AACA) is the largest vintage vehicle club in the world. In 1935, a small group of people with a common interest in old cars formed the organization. Their aim was to gather together to plan outings and driving contests.

As the years passed, the driving contests gave way to contests of skill and workmanship in the restoration of older vehicles. In the spring of 1952, at the AACA National Meet in Pottstown, Pennsylvania, the AACA started judging the quality and authenticity of restoration work.

Competitive judging in AACA events is based on evaluating how closely a vehicle has been restored to the same state as when the dealer received it from the factory. Any feature, option or accessory shown in the original factory literature is acceptable for judging.

Starting in 1958, the AACA established separate classifications for commercial vehicles. Since that time, seven classes in which trucks, ambulances and fire apparatus are judged have been established. The classes are based on the year, load capacity rating and type of vehicle.

James Stewart brought his 1935 Stewart dump truck to Hershey in 1993.

This 1934 Mack "Bulldog" dump truck seen at Hershey worked for the Department of Public Works in Barrington, New York.

Moxley's Seed Service Center promoted its business with this restored Mack platform truck that it brought to Hershey, Pennsylvania.

According to AACA guidelines, "commercial vehicles" are basically trucks and buses of any kind, but not station wagons and taxicabs. Hearses cannot be registered in commercial vehicle classes.

Fire vehicles are classified as self-propelled vehicles for fighting fires. This includes pumpers, chemical wagons, hose trucks, ladder trucks and deluge wagons.

The seven AACA classes that accommodate "trucks" are described as follows:

Number	Years	Type	Load Capacity
22a	Through 1927	Commercial vehicles & ambulances	Under 1-ton
22b	1928-1942	Commercial vehicles & ambulances	Under 1-ton
22c	1943-1968	Commercial vehicles & ambulances	Under 1-ton
22d	Through 1927	Commercial vehicles & ambulances	1-ton or over
22e	1928-1942	Commercial vehicles & ambulances	1-ton or over
22f	1943-1968	Commercial vehicles & ambulances	1-ton or over
23	Through 1968	Fire vehicles	Not specified

Growing interest in the truck collecting hobby has been evidenced by the increasing number and variety of trucks participating in AACA events during the past several years. This trend has been pleasantly obvious at the biggest show of them all ... the club's National Fall Meet in Hershey, Pennsylvania. It takes place in October.

One major push has come from the light-duty truck collectors who restore pickups, sedan deliveries, panel trucks and other models. These are very popular because they combine many of the attractions of larger trucks with the convenience of a "garage-able" size. Some have car-like engineering and convenience features that make them comfortable and easy to drive.

At the other end of the spectrum, there's also been a boom in the collecting of big trucks with unique, special-purpose bodies. It seems that trucks made to do a specific job ... mix cement, deliver soda pop, move household goods, etc. ... are the ones that everyone likes to restore. They can be painted bright colors and decorated with eye-catching lettering and logos. Such trucks really evoke memories. They create excitement and bring out the truck-loving child in all who see them.

For information about the AACA or the AACA Fall National Meet contact the Antique Automobile Club of America, 501 West Governor Road, Hershey, Pennsylvania 17033 or telephone (717) 534-1910.

(John Gunnell is the editorial director of Krause Publication's automotive books department and the editor of the Standard Catalog of American Light-Duty Trucks.)

Attracting lots of admiring looks at Hershey this year was George Schaaf's 1933 Autocar 3-compartment tanker.

Collecting toy trucks

By Frank Malatesta

My interest in what are now considered "classic" toy trucks began when they were new. I was just a boy and my favorite toys were the sturdy trucks built by Fred Lundahl's Buddy L company.

Fred Lundahl started Pressed-Steel Truck Parts Company in 1910, long before I was born. He turned out parts for IHC products, as well as for other trucks and farm machines. Around 1920, the company began making toy trucks. They were named after Fred's son Arthur B. Lundahl.

I played hard with most of my toy trucks. In some cases, this lowered their survival rate. However, those Buddy Ls were made to last. They outlasted my childhood. Eventually, I became involved in the transporting of vintage cars and trucks. Through meeting hobbyists, I discovered that Buddy L toy trucks had become very sought after.

A page from the 1930-1931 Sturditoy catalog.

Many collectors obtain their first classic toy trucks from friends and relatives who know of their appreciation for antiques. Truck drivers are a good source, too. They like trucks and often pick up toy trucks when they travel to different places.

Some of my favorite Buddy Ls include the fire engine, the REA express truck, the auto wrecker and the steam-operated cement mixer. (I also like the number 963 train set, although it is not a truck.)

Keystone toy trucks are another favorite with collectors. Desirable models from this firm include the Bell System utility truck, which is a replica of a Packard. The Keystone tanker truck and parcel post truck are also quite popular.

Other brands of collectible toy trucks include Tonka, Structo, NyLint, Reuhl, Ertl, Doepke, Hubley, Smith-Miller and Sturditoy. An excellent source of information about old toy trucks is Toy Collector and Price Guide, 700 East State Street, Iola, WI 54990. This bi-monthly magazine sells for $2.95 per copy on newsstands. A one-year subscription is $16.95.

This replica toy resembles a full-size antique Packard moving truck that Frank Malatesta owns.

Die cast metal models and metal banks are another option for enthusiasts who enjoy collecting replicas of big trucks. This is the Eastwood "Christmas Delivery Special" produced by Ertl in 1990.

Automotive swap meets (flea markets) are often filled with vending spaces offering old toy trucks for sale.

In addition to toy versions, plastic scale-model kits of big trucks are available. This is Monogram's Snap Tite "Road Hog" model.

Highway Pioneers
1900-1939

"Truck" comes from a Greek word for wheels. Before motor trucks, the term was used to describe wagons, railroad equipment and other devices. Here's a horse drawn ice and coal truck at work for the Cedar Lake Ice Company. (VAE)

A horse drawn Brink's truck carries a load of household effects to someone's new home in the pre-motor truck years. Brink's would later employ many specially-designed motorized trucks in its armored car service. (BAC)

This 1904 Columbia 5-ton truck worked for Montgomery Ward & Company. It was made by the Electric Vehicle Company of Hartford, Connecticut. Two motors could propel it to six miles per hour. It had hard rubber tires. (OCW)

Hammond & Sloane, a New York engineering and contracting firm, put this 1906 Atlas 2-ton truck to work. It used a two-cylinder 24 horsepower gasoline engine. New York was a hotbed of early truck development activities. (NAHC)

Oscar Lear Auto Company of Columbus, Ohio offered the 1-1/2-ton Frayer-Miller truck from 1906-1910. It used a four-cylinder air-cooled engine and sold for $3,000. The 1907 platform/stake could work carrying large, bulky loads. (JW)

Cascarets was the brand name of a candy cathartic (laxative) that used the slogan "They work while you sleep." The work of delivering the product was handled by this 1908 Mitchell 1-1/2-ton express truck. (NAHC)

This "remarkable Rapid" ton car was tested on the 1908 Glidden Tour, in which it carried a 25 percent over-load to challenge its hauling abilities. Rapid made trucks in Detroit (1904-1905) and Pontiac (1905-1912), Michigan. (NAHC)

Two employees of Schrum Brothers' Calumet Pickle Works in Hammond, Indiana, use a 1908 Reliance to get the job done. This 3-1/2-ton Model H has a rack body for carrying high loads. Reliance became part of General Motors. (HAC)

A Goodyear Tire crew in Akron, Ohio poses with Reliance number 1, the first truck in the company's fleet. This was also the first heavy-duty truck used in the city and remained in service from May 25, 1908 to June 6, 1917. (GTC)

While the pilot, co-pilot and navigator sit quiet, but alert in the cab of this 1909 5-ton Mack Manhattan truck, the ground crew loads the vehicle with corn flakes to feed the hungry world. (MTI)

Four workers of the Bowling Green Storage & Van Company ride with their load on a 1909 Couple Gear household moving van in a New Jersey city. Note the old motorcycle propped up against the picket fence behind the truck. (NAHC)

Hard at work for Sheffield Farms is a 1910 Hewitt 10-ton truck. It was one of a fleet of three such commercial vehicles operated by Slawson Decker Company of Brooklyn, New York. This nameplate was later associated with Mack. (MTI)

Helping this 1910 Lansden 8-ton truck do its work were the electric storage batteries located behind the seat and behind the rear axle. This firm produced trucks in four states from 1905 to 1928. (NAHC)

A worker for the Texas Company delivers petroleum products in a 1910 Mack 4-ton tanker. Note the famous red star logo on the side of the cab. Mack started in Brooklyn, New York and moved to Allentown, Pennsylvania. (TA)

Five chaps that look like they "earn their keep" accompany a load of 100-pound sacks being delivered on a 1909 Kato four-wheel drive truck. The sacks are marked Mankato, Minnesota, which is where Kato trucks were built. (MHS)

"The Strenuous Randolph" was the nickname of this large express truck, which covered the 1,700-mile Munsey Tour of 1910. Randolphs were built in Flint, Michigan from 1908 to 1912 and in Chicago during 1912 and 1913. (NAHC)

These well-dressed employees of Universal Motor Truck Company are hard at work driving a 3-ton 1910 Model A stake truck near the firm's Detroit, Michigan headquarters. (NAHC)

The Central Brewing Company used this 5-ton 1911 American platform/stake truck to carry products from its plant near New York City's East River back when delivery men wore jackets and ties. (NAHC)

Well-known John Wanamaker department store employed a 5-ton model built by Commercial Motor Car Company to take products to its customers. The New York City firm also made 1-, 2- and 3-ton trucks between 1906 and 1912. (NAHC)

Warm clothing and goggles were items early truck drivers required to get their work done. These operators are participating in a Chicago newspaper's commercial vehicle test with a 1911 Model C 1-1/2-ton Harder truck. (NAHC)

Carrying number 30 in the 1911 Chicago Evening American Commercial Vehicle Reliability Run was a 1911 Owosso 2-ton with hard rubber tires and chain drive. The gent behind the seat is there to monitor performance. (NAHC)

Grosse Pointe Transit used a 1911 Packard platform/stake truck to get the job done. Note the 1911 Michigan license plate bearing a transit medallion. Though best known for cars, Packard also made trucks from 1905 to 1923. (SPC)

A 1911 Seitz 3-ton stake truck was perfect for carrying kegs of Ideal Beer made by the Independent Brewing Company of Detroit, Michigan. The containers indicate the product was distilled "without drugs or poison." (NAHC)

A small working truck was this 1912 Chase Wire Screen Delivery Wagon. It featured an air-cooled, three-cylinder engine. R.H. Macy & Co. made deliveries from its department store on 34th Street in New York with this vehicle. (HAC)

Clothing made the driver in 1912. This nattily dressed delivery man looks relaxed behind the wheel of his 1912 Durable Dayton Model K 3-ton. This gas-engined truck sold for about $2,250. (DPL)

Loading lath (narrow strips of wood used as a base for plaster walls) into this 1912 Smith-Milwaukee truck was quite a job for these Tews Lime & Cement Company workers. The 3-1/2-ton Model A was made by A.O. Smith Company. (AOS)

A.M. Kingmann & Sons was involved in moving pianos in Brooklyn, New York. Their shiny moving van is a 1912 Velie Model Z 3-ton truck. (NAHC)

This driver didn't have to worry about the weather when he went to work. His 1912 Wilcox Model K 1-1/2-ton stake has a fully vestibuled cab, which came in very handy in Minneapolis, Minnesota where Wilcox trucks were built. (NAHC)

Southern Dairies of Washington, D.C. employed a fleet of 800 vehicles in its dairy business. This 1913 Detroit Electric 2-ton flareboard express advertises the company's "Velvet Kind" ice cream. (OCW)

Working at road improvements is a 1913 Locomobile Model A 5-ton truck from the fleet of Barrett Manufacturing Company of New York. This firm's Tarvia road covering preserved roads and prevented dust. (NAHC)

Showing some signs of its hard working life is a 1912-1913 Sternberg Model 2 2-ton platform truck. This model retailed for $2,800. It was manufactured in Milwaukee, Wisconsin. (OCW)

Part of the Texas company's work-truck fleet was vehicle number A-102, a 1914 GMC Model SC 2-ton tank truck. This model was gasoline powered and listed for $1,900. It was offered from 1913 to 1915. (TA)

Laboring under a huge load of brewery cases and beer kegs is a 1914 Jeffery Quad buttoned up against inclement weather. The driver, employed by Highland Brewing Company of Highland, Illinois, is also well buttoned up. (OCW)

The Knox Martin tractor of 1914 was a three-wheel truck. It was powered by a four-cylinder overhead valve engine that produced 40 horsepower. Such trucks were used to haul two-wheel trailers loaded with goods. (GTC)

This is a 1914 or 1915 (the license plate is of 1915 issue) Peerless 5-ton truck hard at work at a construction site. It was used by the Austin Company, an industrial building firm. Note the right-hand driving position. (HAC)

A road building crew from Polk County, Tennessee poses with its White truck, which is nicknamed "Boss of the Road." The 5-ton Model TKA-ATC gas-powered dump truck is fitted with tractor wheels to get the job done. (WTD)

A 1914 Curtis truck stands outside the Gleason Works, a major supplier of gear manufacturing machinery used to make car and truck rear axles. The Curtis was built by Pittsburgh Machine Tool Company of Braddock, Pennsylvania. (RJG)

The 1914 Curtis 2-ton truck sold for $3,000. It was powered by a 27 horsepower four-cylinder engine. The Gleason Works building in the photo background still exists. It is now totally covered with ivy. (RJG)

Traveling 30,000 miles in a 1915 truck was a grueling experience. That's what the operators of this Denby flareboard express achieved. Denby Motor Truck Company was a Detroit, Michigan firm. This Model B 1-ton cost $1,600. (NAHC)

Betcha the "doughboys" riding inside this hard-rubber-tired 1916 Garford truck had their teeth rattled a bit. The 5-ton Model D cost $4,300 in chassis form. The stake body was extra. Garfords were built in Lima, Ohio. (NAHC)

Goodyear Tire Company used this 1916 IHC screenside delivery to run chores at the Akron, Ohio plant. Note the pneumatic tires and rolled up side curtains. The "French" style sloping hood was an IHC characteristic. (GTC)

Delivering Shell gasoline is a 1917 Hewitt-Ludlow truck. This brand of trucks was manufactured at a factory at 901-951 Indiana Street, in San Francisco, California. Apparently, Shell had a fleet of at least nine such tankers. (JW)

Liberty or USA trucks soldiered valiantly through World War I battlefields. They had a standard design conforming to U.S. Army specifications issued in March 1917. Fifteen different companies produced 9,452 of them. (OCW)

The shovel-nosed Mack truck could work like a bulldog, which it was nicknamed after. This 1917 dump-bodied model is hauling a World War I army tank. (GTR)

Charles Nash purchased Jeffery and put his own name on their Model 2017 truck. He built 3,000 of them in 1917. Rated for one ton, the gas-powered truck chassis was $1,595. The canopy express body added to the total price. (AMC)

One of the most famous old trucks is Goodyear Tire Company's "Wingfoot Express." A 1917 Packard truck was restored to resemble the original. Here it gets a send off from Minnie Mouse on the 1987 Great American Race. (GTC)

Independent Oil Company advertised that there were "none better" than its Oylrite brand lubricants. The company's fleet of tankers included this 1917 Wilcox manufactured by Wilcox Motor Company of Minneapolis, Minnesota. (JW)

Earnest Hoffman's Central Market, in Cedarburg, Wisconsin, used a 1918 Dodge stake bed to make deliveries. In those days, telephone numbers consisted of only three digits that fit easily on the door of this enclosed cab truck.

This 1918 Oneida never worked as hard as it played. Chet Krause, founder of Krause Publications, bought it in the early 1980s with only a few hundred miles showing. It was disassembled when nearly new and stored for 60 years.

A French Legionnaire watches over a fleet of 1918 Nash Quads built for World War I service. During that conflict, these four-wheel drive, four-wheel steer trucks earned an enviable reputation as freedom fighters. (AMC)

The young man on top of the pile relaxes after loading a huge amount of freight on a 1918 Packard platform truck. The Canadian Transport Company Limited operated the 5-ton Model E in pleasant or snowy weather. (NAHC)

J.L. Ware built a truck under his name from 1912 to 1916. He then designed this 2-ton stake bed model for Twin City Four Wheel Drive Company. The firm had two factories, one in Minneapolis and the other in St. Paul. (OCW)

Hard at work in the onion fields is a 1918 Winther-Marwin Model 430 1-1/2-ton truck. The builder of this rig started in Winthrop Harbour, Illinois, but moved to Kenosha, Wisconsin in mid-1918. It features four-wheel drive. (FLP)

Meyers Machine Company of Sheboygan, Wisconsin manufactured Wisconsin trucks from 1915-1918. This tanker was part of the Standard Oil Company fleet and advertises Polarine lubricants for cars and Perfection home heating oil. (JW)

A Dayton Power & Light Company worker poses in the cab of a 1919 Oldsmobile Economy truck. Behind him is the power company's transportation department. A sign says "Drive slow; Sound your Klaxon," referring to the Klaxon horn. (OMD)

Charles D. Peck is the owner of this nicely restored 1919 Oldsmobile 1-ton flareboard express truck. A placard on the side advertises his trucking businesses in Norwalk, Brea and Yorba Linda California. (CPI)

"Your truck for your work," was Oldsmobile's truck sales slogan. This 1919 Economy Truck Express with sill boards sold for $1,350. Oldsmobile made trucks 1904 to 1908; 1918-1924; 1936-1939; and, more recently, from 1991 on. (OCW)

Joy Brothers Motor Car Company sold somebody this handsome, pre-owned 1919 Packard stake bed truck. The license plate indicates the picture was taken during 1922 in Minnesota. The "G" logo on the door is not explained. (OCW)

Art Bennett and his mother participate in the Little Silver, New Jersey firemans' 75th anniversary parade on June 28, 1981. Their 1920 American LaFrance Type 75 won first prize for privately owned fire trucks. (AB)

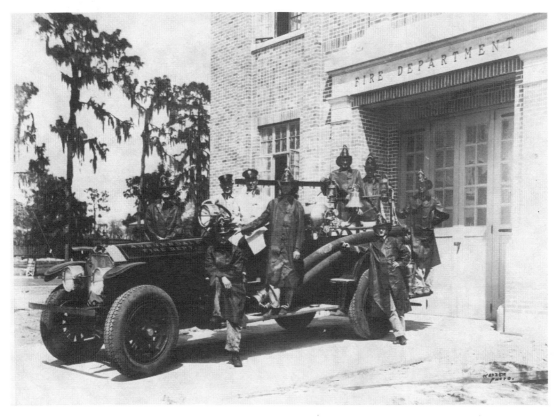

Ready to combat blazes in the town of Auburndale are nine firefighters posing with a 1920 American LaFrance chemical hose wagon. Do you think that this fire house, which looks nearly new, is still in service? (OCW)

Goodyear Tire and Rubber Company continued to work for better roads and improvements in motor truck transport during the 1920s. This 1920 Clydesdale van type truck was nicknamed the "Highway Express." (GTC)

After doing yeoman's duty during World War I, many of the trucks built by the Four Wheel Drive Auto Company of Clintonville, Wisconsin were pressed into utility service. Note the built-in storage bins on this canopy express. (FWD)

Carrying heavy loads was a necessity in the work done by the Ferguson Brothers Manufacturing Company of Hoboken, New Jersey. They used this 1920 General Vehicle company electric truck with an express body. (HAC)

Americans were on the move in the post World War I era and that put lots of big trucks to work in the household transportation business. The Santini Brothers, of Bronx, New York used a four-cylinder 1920 Packard van. (HAC)

This fellow probably worked harder sterilizing every bottle of Coca-Cola on the back of his truck than he did driving the 1920 Mack to his customers' grocery stores in New Orleans. (AA)

Even though the American economy went into a slump when World War I ended, truck production climbed by 97,058 units in 1920. One of the trucks produced that year was this 1920 Oldsmobile 1-ton Economy canopy express truck. (OMD)

More and more American cities and towns made the switch to motorized fire fighting apparatus in the Roaring '20s. This four-wheel drive truck is a 1920 Oshkosh Model A that was purchased by the Oshkosh Fire Department. (OCW)

The Seagrave Company of Columbus, Ohio manufactured this 1920 pumper in 1920. Note the fancy pin-striping and scrollwork that decorate the body and wood spoke wheels. (OCW)

A pair of identical 1920 Stewart trucks labored for the C.H. Gerling Coal, in Milwaukee, Wisconsin. These are most likely Stewart Model 7 2-ton trucks with four-cylinder engines and 156-inch wheelbases. (RFZ)

Tufano's Express and Auto Trucking Corporation served customers in Ozone Park (Queens), New York. Much of the firm's heavy shipping was handled by this 1920 White 5-ton canopy express truck. Hard rubber tires were still common. (WTD)

The Fourth District in Brevard County, Florida used this 1920 White Truck to get roadwork done. The photo identifies the vehicle as a 5-ton model, although it does not seem all that large and heavy-duty. (OCW)

C.B. Witt Wholesale Grocers of Tampa, Florida sold everything from soup to nuts. This 1920 White 3-ton express carries Lipton's tea and coffee, Rub No More soap and powder and Witt's Best flour (better than the rest). (OCW)

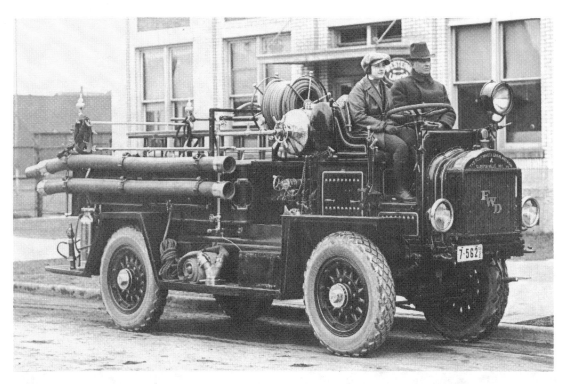

The driver of this 1921 FWD Model B fire truck is a young man of perhaps 16-18 years old. He is parked outside the Western Union office in Clintonville, Wisconsin, where The Four Wheel Drive Auto Company is still located. (FWD)

With few employees, the Gersix Manufacturing Company of Seattle, Washington took nearly a month to make this 1921 Gersix 3-1/2-ton platform truck. Only 100 were built. This one was operated by Curtis Brothers House Movers. (KTC)

There were gasoline shortages in 1921, especially on the West Coast where fuel prices reached 40-cents per gallon. This affected the price of the kerosene being carried by a 1921 Mack tanker owned by Standard Oil Company.

In 1922, truck manufacturers first produced more vehicles with metal wheels than wood wheels. This 1922 Ace moving van had metal wheels, but old-fashioned hard rubber tires. It was built in Newark, Ohio. (LAB)

"Rolling grocery stores" appeared in many American communities during 1922 and prompted grocery store owners to howl. Wholesale grocer Charles H. Moorhouse used this 1922 International for deliveries in Tampa, Florida. (FSU)

This White Model 45 5-ton tanker and tank trailer combination is believed to be of 1923 vintage. It was operated by the Oil Fields Trucking Company of Taft, California. Note the helper wheels behind the dual rear tires. (WTD)

The Fourteenth Avenue Cartage Company took care of General Motors Truck & Coach highway transportation needs, using big rigs like this 1923 GMC 10-ton tractor-trailer combination.It's loaded with 64-pound sacks. (OCW)

Designed especially to carry large loads of vehicle tires, this 1923 MacDonald low-bed truck was used to handle hauling chores at The Universal Tire & Rubber Company's factory in California. Note the dealer plates. (HAC)

The Reliance Fire Proof Door Company of Brooklyn, New York put this 1923 stake rack truck to work hauling its products. This is a 2-1/2-ton model made by Victor Automobile Manufacturing Company of St. Louis, Missouri. (HAC)

Mack continued to offer its AB and AC models for 1924. The AB had a conventional style hood, while the AC (or "Bulldog") style looked like this survivor. ACs came with ratings from 3-1/2-tons to 13-tons. (OCW)

Tractor trailer combinations grew more common to see in many industries in the middle 1920s. This long, two-wheeled trailer was used by a logging company. It's being towed by a circa 1924 FWD truck. (FWD)

Loading brick and tile into the back of this circa 1924 International must have really been back-breaking work. Those were the products of the Georgia and Carolina Brick Company of Florida (Figure that one out!). (FSU)

Three different styles of hardworking 1924 International trucks were operated by Canadian Pacific Express of Toronto, Ontario. This publicity photo comes from Vitralite Automobile Enamel, which was used on 447 trucks in this fleet.

"More miles to the gallon" was promised to customers of Associated Oil Products, which manufactured Cycol Motor Oil. The company used 1924 Kenworth tankers to make its deliveries.

In 1924, production of motor trucks and buses in the United States increased from 409,295 units to 416,659. One of many brands built in Chicago, Illinois was the King Zeitler truck. This one belongs to Canada's Reynolds Museum.

A large Walker electric-powered truck, circa 1925, brought grocers in New York City's Borough of Manhattan their National Biscuit Company cookie and cracker deliveries as late as the spring of 1952, when this photo was snapped.

Workers from the Snow White Laundry Company of Mount Vernon, New York pose with their 1925 Acme 1-1/2-ton truck. The company processed laundry for families, as well as for hotels. The roof rack provided additional room. (HAC)

This good-looking 1925 Corbitt truck was likely a solid worker. It was employed by the Carolina Power & Light Company. Built in Henderson, North Carolina, Corbitts came in eight models ranging from 1- to 5-tons. (NAHC)

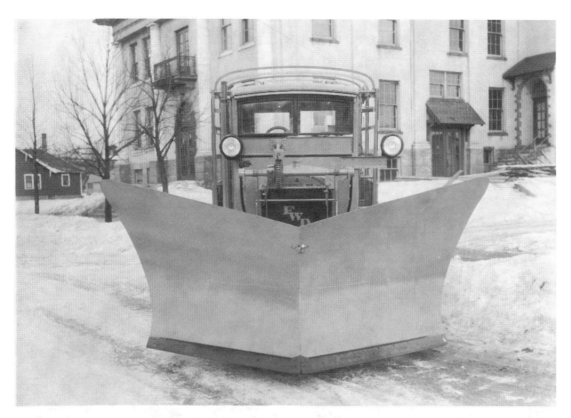

Advances in snow removal were a significant development in the 1920s. This FWD carries a giant V-blade snowplow up front. The structure behind it still stands in Clintonville, Wisconsin. (WPL)

A chapter in the early 1950s book "The Four Wheel Drive Story" (recording the history of FWD Auto Company) deals with the truck-maker's contribution to the development of snow removal equipment, such as this 1925 V-blade plow. (WPL)

The Model 60 Hug Roadbuilder appeared in 1925. It was small, but built for heavy-duty service. About 155 were built through 1931. They were used by road contractors. This particular unit sold for $3,545 f.o.b. Highland, Illinois.

Photo snapped on next-to-last day of 1925 shows a Wisconsin Power & Light work crew with an Oshkosh "4-Wheel-Drive" truck leading another truck, a bus and a car over a snow swept rural road. (WPL)

A shiny 1925 Schacht dump truck labored hard for the W.C. Sellers company of Toledo, Ohio. Logo on hood of the truck bears the name of G.A. Schacht Motor Truck Company and shows city of manufacture as Cincinnati, Ohio. (NAHC)

Frank Radocay, of Milwaukee, Wisconsin, was in the business of general teaming and trucking. This circa 1926 Mack dump truck was one of his sturdier work trucks. Though hardly up-to-date it was up on the job at hand. (PFZ)

Pneumatic truck tires became more popular than solid rubber types for the first time in 1926. This saved millions of road repair dollars. This 1926 Biederman with a Proctor-Keefe tanker body has pneumatics on front. (NAHC)

For 1926, FWD of Clintonville, Wisconsin still offered its 3-ton Model B. This one is outfitted with a canopied utility-express body and a fully-vestibuled cab. The V-blade snowplow blade was a handy wintertime accessory.

Part of Marathon Oil Company's truck fleet was this 1926 International Harvester closed cab truck with a triple-compartment tanker body. The driver's door seems to latch poorly and is tied to a pipe on the side of the tank. (RG)

Though most of its trucks worked as fire fighters, the Luverne Fire Apparatus Company of Luverne, Minnesota also built this moving van in 1926. It was used by M & D Motor Express of Luverne and Sioux Falls, South Dakota. (NAHC)

Breckenridge Material Company of St. Louis, Missouri was established in 1927 and uses this restored 1927 Hug Roadbuilder for advertising and promotions. Interestingly, The Hug Company of Highland, Illinois was founded in 1922. (OCW)

The Willet Company of Chicago, Illinois finished 12 vehicles in its work fleet with Vitralite Automobile Enamel. One was this large 1927 Chicago moving van operated by the Chicago Furniture Manufacturers Association.

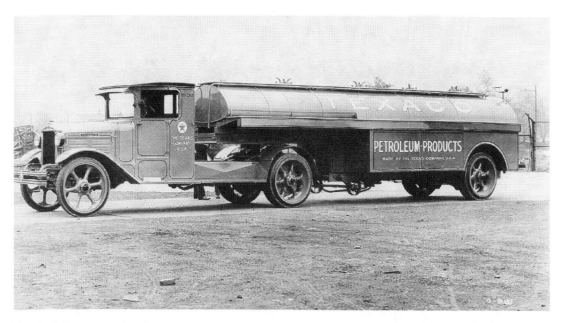

The Heil Company of Milwaukee, Wisconsin, a manufacturer of quality tanks, bodies and hoists, constructed the 2,400-gallon, four-compartment, drop frame trailer tank being pulled by a 1927 Diamond T tractor owned by Texaco. (TA)

Louis Golomb, of Pittsburgh, Pennsylvania, used this specially-bodied 1927 Republic truck in his paints, glass and hardware business. The truck is a 2-ton Model 15. Republic acquired the Linn Tractor Company in 1927. (NAHC)

Purpose-built truck bodies were created to handle all types of special work, such as this 1927 Dodge 1-1/2-ton outfitted for delivery and installation of trees. The body was built by National Steel Products Company. (JE)

Truck production tumbled to its lowest point in five years during 1927. Only 464,793 were built, compared to 608,617 in 1926. This 1927 Larabee closed-cab platform/stake was made by a company in Binghamton, New York. (NAHC)

This restored 1927 Mack AB was seen at a Florida old car show. During 1927, Mack introduced a new work truck powered by a 110-horsepower diesel engine with a Lanova precombustion-chamber cylinder head. (OCW)

Railway Express Agency promised "Safe, sure and fast as ... lightning" delivery with its 1927 Walker electric (top speed 11 miles per hour) truck. This photo was snapped on Stone Street, in New York City, in July, 1952.

Cushman and Sons, a New York City bakery company, painted 480 of its trucks with Vitralite Automobile Enamel. One of them was a 1927 Walker. The Electric Truck Manufacturer's Association was disbanded in 1926 due to declining sales.

This photo shows a number of vintage Walker products still working in the spring of 1952 at Bush Terminal Company in Brooklyn, New York. Note the circa 1927 "Yard Hustler" model pulling a heavily loaded, hard-rubber-tire trailer.

Brockway Motor Truck Company, of Cortland, New York purchased Indiana Truck Company of Marion, Indiana, in 1928 when this Brockway Model R street cleaner was made. Hard rubber tires lost more popularity, but were still seen. (NAHC)

Five Diamond T trucks were added to the fleet of the Makins Construction Company on a snowy day in 1928. They displayed their National Steel Products Company dump bodies in front of Union Station in Kansas City. (JE)

The Fageol Brothers left the American Car & Foundry Company in 1927 to build Twin Coach buses at Kent, Ohio. ACF continued to build trucks with the Fageol name, which it had acquired in 1925. This is the 1928 "Flyer" 1-1/2-ton stake.

T.Eaton Company, Limited of Toronto, Canada operated a 329-vehicle fleet that was painted with Vitralite Automobile Enamel. It included this handsome 1928 GMC screenside delivery used in a "Santa Claus in Toyland" sales promotion.

Linn trucks were half-tracks useful as either load-carriers or tractors. They were particularly well-suited for snowplowing, logging, mining and construction work. They were built in Morris, New York. This is a 1928 model.

Tom Tallman of Jackson, Michigan took a first in class award at an antique auto show with his restored 1928 Reo fire truck. The markings seem to indicate that this Lansing-built open cab pumper was once used in the city of Detroit.

Hand Hoist Dump Body. Quick-acting roller mechanism. Body measurements: length 74", width 52", sides 12" high.

A hand-hoist dump body with quick-acting roller mechanism is seen on this 1928 Rugby 1-ton truck. It is 74 inches long, 52 inches wide and has 12 inch high sides. The Rugby was related to the Star Four made by W.C. Durant. (JG)

A load of new 1928 model Chevrolets arrives at Cipperly & Knapp Motor Company's dealership on the back of a White tractor trailer. A total of 6,260 White commercial vehicles were sold during 1928. (OCW)

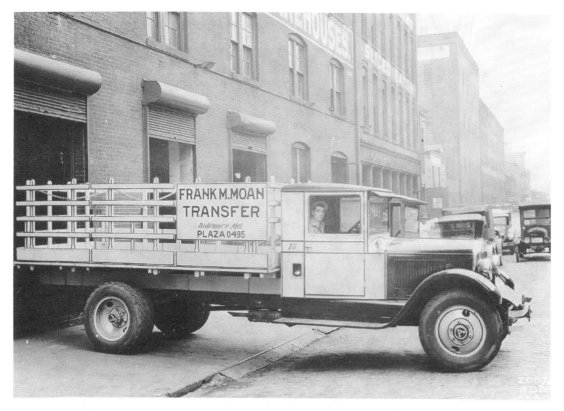

A 1929 Autocar was the work truck preferred by Frank M. Moan Transfer of Baltimore, Maryland. This manufacturer was located in Ardmore, Pennsylvania from 1908 to 1954, when it became a division of White Motor Company. (NAHC)

Hess Express of Fox Chase, Pennsylvania used a 1929 Day-Elder truck in its delivery business. Day-Elder revised its vehicles in 1929, introducing a new "Super Service Six" series in capacities from 1-ton to 6-tons. (NAHC)

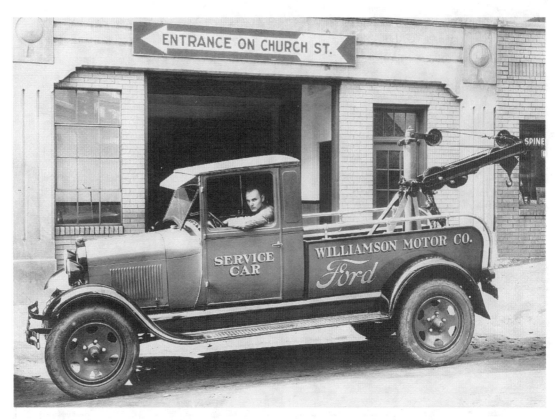

All-steel welded road service bodies were first made available for the Ford truck chassis in 1929. This Model AA Ford service car was operated by Williamson Motor Company on Church Street in New York City. (AA)

Set up for heavy-duty service with tandem rear axles and a frame extension is a 1929 Ford Model AA truck. It is fitted with a high rack body for the hauling of auto parts and tires by Frank Breska, an authorized Ford dealer. (AA)

Working hard in a logging operation in the State of Washington is a 1929 International tractor-trailer. By 1929, International had expanded to 170 branches and production reached a record of 50,000 trucks for the year. (TT)

Well-known truck collector Frank Malatesta brought his 1929 Mack AC "Bulldog" platform/stake bed truck to the Antique Automobile Club of America's 1992 Fall National Meet in Hershey, Pennsylvania. (JAG)

Goodyear pneumatic tires were mounted on this 1929 Sterling truck that worked for the Milwaukee Gas Light Company in Wisconsin. Sterlings were built there from 1916 to 1952 under three different corporate arrangements. (PFZ)

J.V. Miller and his son pose with their 1929 Studebaker 2-ton truck. Miller operated a Studebaker bus line in Owen Sound, Ontario, Canada prior to moving to LaGlace (400 miles north of Edmonton, Alberta) with his truck in 1933. (CN)

Although not a mainline maker of fire-fighting apparatus, Studebaker turned out a number of handsome fire trucks from its South Bend, Indiana factory. This 1929 model is getting the once over from a proud fire chief. (AA)

McColl Frontenac Oil Company, Limited used a 1929 Studebaker service truck to do chores and make deliveries. Studebaker offered three body heights and four load lengths (13 body choices in all) in three six-cylinder lines. (AA)

"Cook by wire" Interstate Power & Light advertised on the side of its 1930 Ford Model AA utility van. Rural electrification was one of the most important jobs being tackled by American workers in this era. (OCW)

Workers at National Steel Products Company built the heavy-duty dump body for this 1930 Indiana Six. This brand of trucks was built in Marion, Indiana through 1933, when the company moved to Cleveland, Ohio. (JE)

An International truck from the Smith, Richardson & Conroy Company fleet. This one has a rack body with curtain-sides and a screen-divided compartment (probably for safeguarding the Budweiser beer.)

Carnation Farm Products brought its goods to market in this 1930 Kenworth 10-ton articulated van. The graphics show pickle cheese, butter, pasteurized milk, certified milk, whipping cream, cottage cheese and ice cream. (KTC)

Relay Motors Corporation was in its fourth year of operations when this hefty 1930 Relay 4-ton dump truck was manufactured. It had a powerful Buda six-cylinder engine and a four-speed transmission. (NAHC)

Loading lumber was hard work, but this 1930 Reo Speedwagon was a big help when it came to delivering the goods to customers. It was used by employees of Kimball & Prince Lumber Company in Vineland, New Jersey. (OCW)

Workers load barrels into the back of a 1930 Schacht 3-ton enclosed cab truck with flareboard express body. They were employees of the Hudepohl Brewing Company in Cincinnati, Ohio, where Schachts were built. (NAHC)

In 1930, Studebaker and Pierce-Arrow announced a new joint venture known as SPS Truck Corporation to handles sales and marketing of both brands. This is a 3-1/2-ton model used by the Coca-Cola Bottling Company. (AA)

White also supplied smaller beverage delivery trucks to Coca-Cola Bottling Company. This one appears to be a medium-duty 2-1/2-ton enclosed cab model. It wears 1930 Texas license plates. (AA)

Railcar maker American Car & Foundry went into the transit car business in 1925 and built the model TT175 articulated truck in 1930. This one was employed by Atlantic States Transfer Corporation for Eastern seaboard runs.

American highway building went on during the depression, using vehicles such as this 1931 FWD dump truck and grader. The four-wheel drive running gear was well-suited to roadway construction work. (NAHC)

Starting in 1931, some states began to allow only trucks with pneumatic tires on highways. This 1931 Gramm 8-ton articulated truck was even equipped with a sleeper cab for long-distance hauling. (NAHC)

During 1931, Pierce-Arrow re-entered the truck market with six models of 2-ton to 8-ton capacity. Michael J. Torpey's contracting company, located in Woodside, Long Island, New York, used this 1931 Pierce-Arrow 5-ton dump truck.

A total of 432,262 trucks were made during depression year 1931. It was the seventh year in a row of sluggish sales. That made this Studebaker medium-duty 2-compartment tanker rare. It was owned by Kemp Oil Company of Dallas, Texas.

The end of the line was approaching in 1931, when this Ward 4-ton electric van was sold to Windsor Dairy Farm to deliver Meadow Gold Ice Cream in Colorado. Ward had only three more years left in the truck business. (NAHC)

Nine million people drank Coca-Cola in 1931, when the beverage company purchased this White bottle truck to make deliveries to its wholesale customers. (AA)

115

This 1932 Chevrolet rig fits that "a case of good judgment" slogan on the side of the trailer. It was a great tractor trailer outfit for hauling Edelweiss beer. Note that the lettering "since '52" means 1852! (AA)

Texaco employed this handsome 1932 Diamond T 1500-gallon 5-compartment 6 x 4 tanker to make deliveries. Here we see it parked at Diamond T Motor Car Company's service department facility in Chicago, Illinois. (TA)

Part of the load on this trailer truck is a new Coca-Cola product called "Five-O." The rig is a 1932 International. During this year, the American Association of State Highway Officials adopted truck size and weight limits.

Siebert's Motor Haulage of Palisades Park, New Jersey hauled dairy products for Middletown Milk & Cream Company of Slate Hill, New York using a Mack AP 15-ton articulated van. Note the 1932 New Jersey license plates. (NAHC)

The Federal Motor Carrier Act of 1932 gave the Interstate Commerce Commission regulatory powers over interstate trucks. That included this 1932 White sleeper cab tractor trailer owned by Central Freightways, Incorporated. (WTD)

This 1932 White beverage truck toiled for the Coca-Cola Bottling Works of Bethlehem, Pennsylvania. In 1932, White Motor Company announced it would start marketing trucks assembled by Indiana Truck Corporation through its dealers.

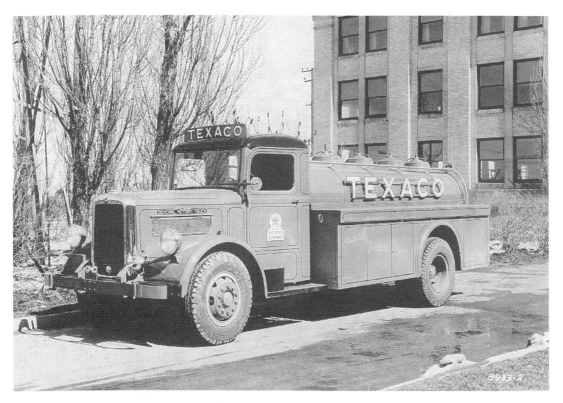

In 1933, commercial vehicle production in the United States took a slight leap up to 329,218 units. One of them was this work-ready 4-compartment tanker that General Motors Truck (GMC) turned out for the Texas Company. (TA)

A big boost for Hendrickson of Lyons, Illinois came in 1933. International Harvester, of Chicago, agreed to use its tandem suspension system. This 1933 Hendrickson 10-ton 6 x 4 van and closed trailer was a typical example. (HAC)

Trucking safety was a concern in 1933. Thirty-nine states limited driving hours. In addition, trucks like this 1933 Kenworth 6 x 4 tractor with 3-axle trailer had to have "Inflammables" signs when carrying dangerous loads. (KTC)

"This new truck delivers a larger quantity of higher quality with more quickness," says the lettering on the side of this 1933 Mack Model BJ 5-ton grain box truck. Only 1,862 of these rigs were made from 1927 to 1933. (MTC)

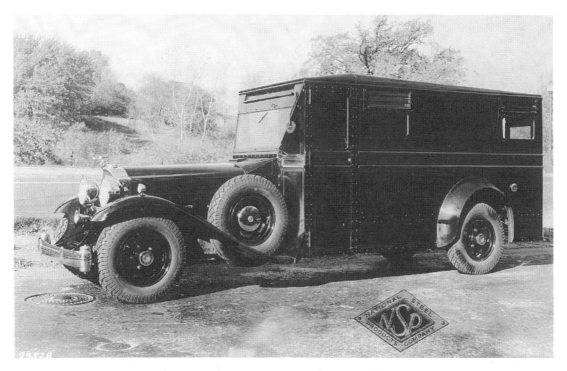

In 1933, the National Steel Products Company produced this armored truck on a Packard chassis. Packard also built trucks up to 2-ton capacity between 1905 and 1923. (JE)

In addition to its big trucks and semis, Coca-Cola used smaller rigs for other jobs. Here we see a 1933 White Panel Delivery emblazoned with the beverage company's slogan, "Drink Coca-Cola: delicious and refreshing." (AA)

A participant in the 1990 Great American Race was this 1934 Dodge platform/stake truck nicknamed "The Blarney Wagon." Dodge added a new 1-1/2-ton model to its line during 1934. (OCW)

The V-8 emblems on this 1934 Ford truck distinguish it from the similarly styled 1933 model. It is parked outside a Kentucky Ford and Fordson tractor garage selling Kyso and Standard gasoline. It was torn down in 1938. (JA)

The American Trucking Association fought for the right for self-regulation in 1934, when this GMC Model T-74HC 12-ton truck with sleeper cab was made. Here we're beginning to see a hint of streamlined cab design. (GMC)

Texaco "Fire-Chief" Ethyl gas, Indian gas, Texaco "Fire-Chief" gas and Havoline oil were delivered to this station by a 1934 GMC tanker. Price for the regular (first pump) was 15-cents per gallon, plus a 4-1/2-cents tax. (TA)

A trio of Brink's Incorporated armed security guards pose proudly by their new 1934 International armored car outside a new Sears, Roebuck and Company store in Chicago, Illinois. This was Brink's 75th year of service since 1859.

Pacific Refrigerating Company offered ice and cold storage. It used this International C Line tractor trailer on runs from Kent, Washington to Tacoma. Lettering on the door of the cab indicates, "Under 50,000 gross." (TT)

A pair of 1934 Mack Model BC 5-compartment 1,200-gallon trucks ready to go to work delivering fuel. These 7-ton, 6 x 4 tankers featured a big six-cylinder engine. (TA)

Gargoyle Mobiloil and Mobilgas were the well-known products of the Socony-Vacuum Company. Here we see a White Star Refining Company employee at work filling a 1934 Studebaker Model W8 4-compartment tanker with Mobilgas. (AA)

Borden's Farm Products Company used fender-skirted trucks to get ice cream to retailers in California. This is a 1934 Studebaker Model T641 refrigerated delivery truck. Borden's Associated Companies was formed in 1857. (AA)

Promoted as the 2,000-mile oil," Kendall lubricants were distributed by Thomas Mairs in the Utica, New York area using a 1934 Studebaker Model T665 delivery van. (AA)

T.Miles Oil Company was a distributor of Texaco products in the Indianapolis, Indiana area. Deliveries were made using a home-state-built 1934 Studebaker Model T641 5-compartment tanker truck. (AA)

Ebling Brewing Company's brew was promoted as "That Grand Old Beer." The New York City company pressed this 1934 Studebaker Model T441 stake-express truck into service carrying large loads of heavy wooden beer kegs. (AA)

The M. O'Neil Company of Akron, Ohio relied on this reliable 1934 White furniture van to carry its client's household goods to their new home. Here we see two employees unloading a desk from the truck. (MOC)

"Thirst knows no season," a new Coca-Cola slogan, is advertised on this 1934 White-Indiana Beverage truck. Indiana was now being operated as a subsidiary of the well-known Cleveland, Ohio truck manufacturer. (AA)

This big 1935 3-ton Dodge was used by the Texas Company at its New Jersey storage facility. We're not certain if the body is of an unusual tanker style or a panel side express. Does anyone reading this book know? (AA)

Virtually identical to Dodge trucks marketed in the United States was the badge-engineered Fargo line offered in Canada. This is a 1935 Fargo that worked for Canadian National Express Company. (RPZ)

Great Southern Trucking Company operated in Florida, Georgia, North Carolina, South Carolina, Alabama and Tennessee offering warehouse cold storage and refrigerated delivery service. The company used a 1935 Ford tractor trailer.

Gulf Refining Company transported its refined products to market in a handsome-looking 1935 GMC Model T-16 3-ton truck and trailer. The Interstate Commerce Commission created a division to regulate motor trucks in 1935. (GMC)

In the city of Twin Falls, Idaho a 1934 Studebaker tank truck helped keep the streets clean. Commercial vehicle output climbed again in 1935, peaking at 697,367 trucks for the calendar year. (AA)

The ICC's Washington, D.C.-based Motor Carrier Division, new for 1935, anticipated opening 15-20 district offices nationwide to regulate the trucking industry. Trucker J.E. Robertson used a Model 1W841 Studebaker to haul ale.

"Vas you efer in Zinzinnati?" was the slogan decorating this 1935 Studebaker Model W841 tractor truck and trailer. The 7,750-pound trailer had a 2-1/2-ton capacity with 8.25 x 20 tires in front and 9.00 x 20 in the rear. (AA)

The steady increase of truck building continued in 1936, when annual production climbed to 782,220 vehicles. This 1936 cab-over-engine Autocar 2-compartment tanker was operated by Behrens Brothers Fuel Service. (AA)

"Stop-wear" lubrication service was offered by this Union 76 garage in a town called Marysville. The Western Oil and Burner Company used a 1936 Chevrolet tanker with fender skirts to carry its products. (OCW)

Diamond T displayed a light diesel truck at the 1936 Chicago truck show. This restored 1936 Diamond T tractor appeared at the 1992 old car show in Iola, Wisconsin, the hometown of Krause Publications. (RK)

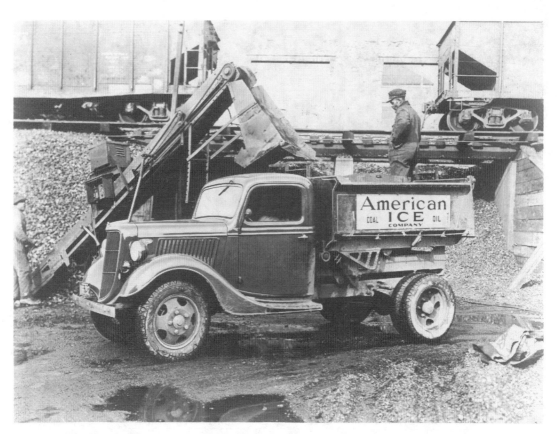

Working for the American Ice Company is a 1936 Ford dump truck chassis and cab with a high-lift coal body. Dual rear wheels were standard on this short wheelbase model. It had a base price of $638 with hydraulic springs optional.

Railway Express Agency offered advertising on the sides of its delivery trucks. This 1936 International carries a message promoting "25 percent more California Sunkist oranges for your money." Sounds like a "sweet, juicy" deal!

Carrying a load of hay is a 1936 International Model C-30 stake/rack model. This was a 1-1/2-ton truck and had a base chassis price of just $610. It used IHC's smaller six-cylinder engine. The chassis weight was 3,038-pounds. (AA)

Tri-City Packing Company of Davenport, Iowa dealt in quality meats, fresh fruits and vegetables and groceries. Deliveries were made with this 1936 Model 20MB Mack Jr. The company served customers in Silvis, East Moline and Geneseo.

Homer W. Fitterling, a well-known collector of antique autos, operated this 1936 Studebaker tractor-trailer. He was sole operator of a direct-line freight service between South Bend, Indiana and St. Louis, Missouri. The run took 13 hours, moving loads faster than rail or the U.S. Mail did at the time. (AA)

Litzelman & Morrison of Indianapolis, Indiana sold this Studebaker S-2673 tractor and Edwards A-3 drop frame semi-trailer to the Edgerton Manufacturing Company of Paoli, Indiana. The rear of the body had five-foot sections that were removable to meet state law restrictions in several regions. (AA)

Gross Brothers Movers of Wisconsin Rapids, Wisconsin used a 1936 Studebaker S-2463 tractor purchased from Thom Automobile Company of Oshkosh, Wisconsin. The 22-foot trailer carries a 25-foot "Aeroflow" streamline van body by Barkow of Milwaukee, Wisconsin. This rig had power brakes and 8.25 x 20 tires. (AA)

A 1936 Studebaker tractor and Keystone trailer carried Heileman's Old Lager beer off to customers in Kansas City, Missouri. The Metro cab-over-engine truck is a Model 2M601. (AA)

J.S. Leonard, a salesman for Issac Fass, Incorporated of Portsmouth, Virgina sold Southern, Piel's, Trommer's, Free State and Sunshine beers and ales. His 1936 Studebaker Model 2M625 cab-over-engine beer truck featured a stake/rack type cargo body and dual rear wheels. (AA)

This short-wheelbase beer wagon is a 1936 Studebaker Model 2M201 Metro cab-over-engine truck. It delivered Esslinger's Beer in the Philadelphia, Pennsylvania area.

A 1936 Studebaker Model 2M225 bottle truck served the Coca-Cola Bottling Company of Alliance, Ohio. Signage on the side of the streamlined body promoted the 50th anniversary of America's "pure as sunlight" soft drink. (AA)

George Shook of Detroit hauled Old Frankenmuth beer in a Fruehauf trailer pulled by a 1936 Studebaker sleeper cab tractor. Interstate truckers in 1936 faced different sets of regulations in all 48 states and Washington, D.C. (AA)

Here's a 1936 Studebaker beverage truck used by a Coca-Cola Bottling franchise in Philadelphia, Pennsylvania. It's a Model 2M225. Studebaker Metro COEs were offered in Boss or Ace models.

Judging by the license plate and number on the cab sill, this is the same 1936 Studebaker Coke truck in Philadelphia. Sign in grocery store window for Lifebouy Soap says, "Stops 'BO' and it's so kind to my skin." (AA)

Studebaker trucks came in many style, model and body configurations in 1936. Shown here is Kenmore Builders Supply's Model 2M201 cab-over-engine stake truck on a short-wheelbase dump truck chassis with dual rear wheels. (AA)

George Nestler Stores, with four locations in Brooklyn, was an upscale New York City furniture retailer. Carpets, rugs, linoleum, beds and bedding were delivered with a fender-skirted 1936 Studebaker Model 2M225 COE truck. (AA)

Wallace Brothers' Studebaker, of Spokane, Washington, sold this 1936 Model 2M225 to General Paint Corporation in the same city. The special body built by Novelty Carriage Works, of Spokane, was designed to carry paint. It is 11-feet long, 6-feet wide and 4-1/2-feet high. Size 7.50 x 20 tires are fitted. (AA)

The Chicago Autocar Branch delivered this rig to L.C.L. Transit Company of De Pere, Wisconsin in 1936. It features a Model 2M-601 Deluxe Studebaker cab with Eaton 2-speed axle. Tires are 8.25 x 20s in front and dual 9.00 x 20s at rear. L.C.L. was a contract hauler for Kraft's Phenix Cheese Company. (AA)

Though it should, perhaps, be in front of the U.S. Treasury Building, this fender-skirted 1937 Autocar armored truck used by the Bureau of Engraving and Printing is actually parked outside the U.S. Department of Agriculture. (OCW)

Production output by the American truck building industry climbed to 891,016 units for calendar 1937. This Autocar dump truck was used by county workers in Stark County, Ohio. (AA)

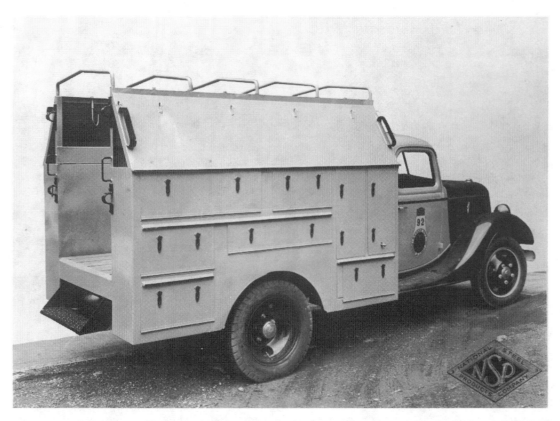

National Steel Products Company, of Kansas City, made this multi-cabinet utility body for a 1937 Ford truck used by the Kansas City Power & Light Company. (JE)

Security Armored Service Company of Kansas City, Missouri contracted with National Steel Products Company to construct this streamlined armored car on a 1937 Ford chassis. It has 1937 Missouri truck license plates. (JE)

Pacific Intermountain Express operated in California, Nevada, Utah, Idaho, Montana, Colorado and Wyoming when this 1937 Kenworth Model 346C 10-ton truck was hauling refrigerated trailers. It is pictured near the Golden Gate Bridge. This "shovel-nose" tractor sold for $9,500. (KTC)

A streamlined Mack EHV with fully-skirted rear fenders delivered Coca-Cola cases in 1937. The six-cylinder EH cab-over-engine chassis cost $2,095. It had a shipping weight of 6,000-pounds and an 18,000-pound load capacity. (AA)

"Serve Coca-Cola at Home" urged the message on this Mack Model 21M bottle truck. It had a chassis price of just $835, including a six-cylinder engine with 3-5/8 x 4-1/4 inch bore and stroke and 27.34 SAE horse-power. (AA)

Maxim is a well-known producer of fire truck apparatus from Middleboro, Massachusetts. This 1937 Model M-3 open cab fire engine must have given fire fighters in the snow belt a cool ride. It was used in Rockville. (MMC)

Ward's "soft bun" bread was delivered in this 1937 Studebaker J30M truck. This 3- to 4-ton COE model used a 4-1/2 x 4-1/2 inch bore and stroke six that produced 43.35 SAE horsepower. The basic chassis sold for $1,930. (AA)

This 1937 Studebaker worked for the U.S. Army. During 1937, this South Bend, Indiana manufacturer added a diesel-engine series to its truck-line. Offered with three wheelbases, the new model featured a Hercules DJXB engine. (AA)

A 1937 Studebaker J20 4-compartment tanker takes on cans of motor oil in a side compartment while parked near Linco Lubrication in an unidentified Indiana town. This 2- to 3-ton model had a $990 chassis price. (AA)

Cities Service Oil Company put this 1937 Studebaker J20 to work making deliveries to a small-town Wisconsin service station. These trucks used a 3-5/8 x 4-1/4 inch six that generated 31.54 SAE horsepower. Dual rear wheels were standard equipment on the three J20 models and the three J20Ms. (AA)

Studebaker's big 3- to 4-ton J30M model was perfectly-suited for carrying this heavy load of hollow building tiles for Alton Brick Company. J30s used the 4-1/2 x 4-1/2 inch, 43.35 horsepower engine and came standard with dual wheels. The M suffix indicated "Metro" (cab-over-engine) styling. (AA)

Streamlining was in vogue on late 1930s trucks, as illustrated by the skirted stake/express body on this 1937 Studebaker J15. The J15M was rated for 1-1/2 to 2-tons and used a 3-1/2 x 4-3/8 inch six with 25.35 SAE horsepower. Prices were $715 to $785 for the dual rear wheels chassis. (AA)

There was a lot of work in the Coca-Cola fleet for Studebaker trucks in 1937. This one is a 1-1/2- to 2-ton Model J-15M. New safety regulations enacted this year required two headlamps, one taillamp and one stoplamp on all trucks. (AA)

"Ask us about the Atlas budget plan," invites the banner on this old Sohio filling station. Do you think the 1937 Studebaker 4-compartment tanker has Atlas tires, too? Sign on truck advertises new Red Crown gasoline.

14th St. Drug Company takes a Coke delivery from the driver of a 1937 White Model 802 truck with full-skirted rear fenders. This COE model was rated 1-1/2-tons and had a $995 chassis price. It used a 3-3/8 x 4-1/8 inch six-cylinder engine. This must be a holiday season photo. The Rx sign advertises box candy for 89-cents and electric wreaths for 29-cents. (AA)

Chemicals were the product carried in this 1938 Autocar stake rack truck that worked for A.H. Mathieu & Company, a chemicals firm in Everett, Massachusetts. In 1938, the ICC determined the average truck driver was 5-foot 8-inches tall, 33 years old and had 13.6 years of driving experience. (AA)

151

"Phill-up with Phillips 66" is the slogan emblazoned on this 1938 Dodge 6-compartment tanker that worked at an Illinois refinery. Dodge used the term "Econ-o-miser" to stress the low operating costs its truck buyers reported.

A 1938 Ford 8 x 2 cab-over-engine redi-mix truck with a Rex motomixer made by the chain belt company of Milwaukee, Wisconsin. It is working for the Grand Trunk Western Railroad and appears to have Pennsylvania license plates. (AA)

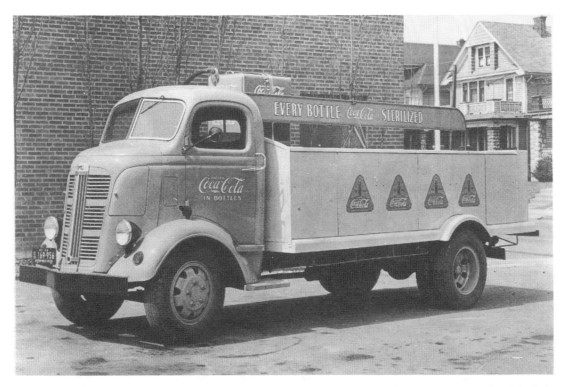

The Automobile Manufacturers Association studied truck fleets in 1938, finding that more than 34 of the top 149 operated in New York City, where this 1938 GMC cab-over-engine Coca-Cola truck worked. It has special 1938 license plates promoting the upcoming 1939-1940 New York World's Fair. (AA)

Though not yet involved in conflicts evolving in European nations, American truck makers found themselves cranking out more and more military vehicles in the late 1930s. This is a 1938 GMC cargo-bodied military model. (AA)

A 1938 International Coca-Cola truck model DS-300. Based on the D-300, it has cab-over-engine styling. Both models used the same 3-5/16 x 4-1/2 inch bore and stroke six-cylinder engine with 26.34 SAE horsepower. The DS (Was S for streamlined or skirts?) weighed about 100 pounds more than a D. (AA)

Atlantic Coal Company employed this 1938 Mack coal truck. The Model EE was a 6-ton with a 3-1/2 x 4-1/8 inch bore and stroke six that gave 75 horsepower at 2800 rpm. The chassis, priced at $935, weighed 4,650 pounds. (AA)

Doyle-Gulf "hired" this snub-nose 1938 Mack six-wheel 3-compartment tanker to make fuel oil deliveries. The Allentown, Pennsylvania truck maker introduced six brand new COE models this season, bringing some out at midyear. (AA)

Dr. Pepper was "good for life" and this 1938 Mack gave cases of the beverage (plus 7-Up) the ride of their life. This is a Model EE 6-ton Mack with skirted rear fenders. (AA)

Mobilgas and Mobiloil were handled by the American Distributing Company of Everett, Massachusetts. The firm used this streamlined 1938 Studebaker tanker to deliver the goods. The K-30 was a 3-ton model. This seems to be the largest version with a 184-inch wheelbase. It had a $2,035 chassis price. (AA)

A 1938 Studebaker K-30 Pennzoil truck with a stake/cargo body at a California refinery. This appears to be the mid-sized 166 inch wheelbase edition (also $2,035). K-30s had a 4-3/4 x 4-1/2 inch six with 43.35 SAE horsepower. (AA)

Better technology led to improvements in the manufacture of insulated and refrigerated bodies during 1938. The Sanitary Sausage Company, of Minneapolis, Minnesota, had such a body mounted on its 1-ton Studebaker K-10 truck with dual rear wheels. A 26.35 SAE horsepower six was used in the K-10. (AA)

South Bend, Indiana's Bituminous Material Distributor used this K-30M Studebaker to blacktop highways in 1938. The "M" in the model designation indicated a COE "Metro" model and K-30 indicated 3-tons. The K-30M came with 101-, 142- and 166-inch wheelbases at chassis prices from $1,935 to $2,035. (AA)

Another Dodge Truck user was White House Quality Meat Market, a Chicago, Illinois grocer connected to the National Tea Company. These workers are delivering a shipment of 7-Up to the store in a 1939 bottle van. The beverage was distributed by Joyce 7-Up, of Joliet. (AA)

Wearing 1939 Illinois license plates is a 1939 Dodge beer delivery van operated by the Schamberger Brothers. Schlitz, "the beer that made Milwaukee famous," was available in both bottles and cans. Note the roof rack. (AA)

Brink's Incorporated had this armored car constructed to its specifications on a 1939 International truck chassis. It has Illinois tags and was probably used near Brink's Chicago headquarters. The fender skirts were functional, giving the rear tires additional protection from bullets. (BAC)

During 1939, International Harvester sent two display trailers coast-to-coast promoting its trucks. Perhaps that inspired Mobiloil to purchase this sleekly streamlined Model D30 1-1/2-ton tanker. The blending of headlamps into the front fenders was a new styling trend. How about those wide whitewalls? (AA)

A 1939 Mack Model EHU bottle truck working for Coca-Cola. This cab-forward model (as Mack described its COEs) utilized a 3-5/8 x 5 inch six-cylinder engine of 31.50 SAE horsepower. This chassis weighed 6,050 pounds and sold for $2,320. The aftermarket beverage delivery body work was extra. (AA)

A variety of beverages were distributed by G. Guarnieri of West 19th Street in New York City and delivered with a 1939 Mack. At the 1939 World's Fair in New York, a fleet of 107 trucks traveled 60,000 miles per month to keep the exposition supplied with goods and necessities. (AA)

Socony Vacuum Oil Company's Lubrite Division put this 1939 Mack to work. It is pictured here at a Mack production or repair facility. The truck is a Model EF 7-tonner with a 290 cubic inch 85 horsepower six-cylinder motor. (AA)

"Serve Coca-Cola at home, ice cold," soda drinkers were advised in 1939, when this Mack EEU cab-forward truck delivered their favorite drink. A 253 cubic inch six developing 75 horsepower at 2800 rpm was under the stubby cab. (AA)

Peterbilt introduced its first trucks in 1939, following T.A. Peterman's purchase of the Fageol factory in Oakland, California. The truck in this photo is identified as a 1939 model with a 6 x 4 chassis, although it seems to have a postwar style bumper.

"No riders" were allowed on this 1939 Studebaker used by General Petroleum Corporation of California. It has license plates promoting the California World's Fair or Golden Gate Exposition. The special cargo body was designed to carry large containers of Mobilgas products. (AA)

Knights of the Road
1940-1969

Production of trucks and buses in 1940 hit 754,901. This 1940 Dodge 1-1/2-ton cab-over-engine stake truck was powered by a 3-3/8 x 4-1/2-inch six-cylinder engine that put out 27.34 SAE horsepower. (OCW)

Two American institutions ... Coca-Cola and Ford ... worked together to quench the thirst of customers at Poss' Barbeque Pig Sandwiches store. Judging by the license plate, the store was in Georgia and the year was 1940. (AA)

Pepsi came in quart-size "Par-T-Paks" from a Michigan beverage distributor who used this 1940 Ford Type 86 cab-over-engine stake truck with rack extensions. This model truck sold for $1,010 complete and weighed 4,376 pounds. The truck also delivered Nehi and Set-Up brand soft drinks. (AA)

Ford offered its largest truck line ever in 1940, with 42 varieties using six wheelbase lengths and three flat-head V-8 engines. Highway tractors, like this one used by Rea & Derick, Incorporated to ship drugs, typically came with the 3.187 x 3.75 inch motor that developed 95 horsepower at 3600 rpm. (AA)

Elmstrom Home Heating Company used this big 1940 Hendrickson dump truck to haul coal. This Chicago company offered 19 models in five lines in 2- to 10-ton capacities with gas or diesel engines. Prices for the chassis ranged from $1,575 up to $8,950 for a 5-ton diesel six-wheeler. (HAC)

A 1940 Reo with a refrigerated van body delivered prime meats and poultry for Sanford Hotel Supply Company of New York City. Reos were built in Lansing, Michigan and had 19 models in five series for 1940. This truck is in the 2- to 3-ton range, where a 3-1/2 x 4-1/4-inch six with 80 horsepower was used. (AA)

"Famous Berghoff Beer" sold by Ziegler & Towner of Lansing, Michigan rode in a 1940 Reo. It seems to be a Model 20B with a 146-inch wheelbase and standard dual rear tires. The chassis cost $1,178 and weighed 4,445 pounds. (AA)

Reo also offered the Model 20A for 1940. It had a 120-inch wheelbase and a chassis price of $1,142. Bodies, such as this low-side dump, were extra. Size 6.00 x 20 tires were used up front, with dual 32 x 6 eight-ply tires on the rear. This truck worked for the City Engineering Department in Lansing. (AA)

Trimble Springs Bottling Company of Colorado distributed Pepsi Cola, 7-Up and other beverages made with mountain spring water in this 1940 Reo beverage delivery truck. (AA)

Earl's Commercial Garage dabbled in many automotive ventures from machine work, welding and towing to selling Studebakers and Reos. The Connecticut sales and service emporium sold this 1940 Reo furniture van to the Champlin Box Company of Hartford. It is a 165-inch wheelbase Model 20C. (AA)

Pamahasika's Performing Pets advertised "Our dogs fed exclusively on Ken-L-Ration, the dog food of champions!" PPP also used a champion American truck produced by Reo Motor Car Company. During 1940, Reo also received an order to build 300 military trucks for the United States Army. War was on the horizon!

The Tennessee Valley Authority used these 1940 Reo Model 21B oil tankers on its construction projects. The 21 designation indicated Reo's 2-1/2-ton line and the B indicated the mid-size 145-inch wheelbase. The 21B chassis tipped the scales at 4,945 pounds and sold for $1,479. (AA)

Trans-Oil Incorporated towed a tank trailer with a 4-ton Series 23 Reo tractor. It appears to be a Model 23B, with the 145-inch wheelbase. A larger 3-5/8 x 5-inch six was used in this line. It produced 93 brake horsepower at 2700 rpm. This truck had a base price of $2,503. (AA)

Reliable Transit Motor Freight Carriers of Illinois operated this 1940 Reo tractor and semi-trailer. "Ship by Truck," the carrier advertised on the side of the trailer. During 1940, the Society of Automotive Engineers recommended that maximum horsepower of trucks be a measure of load-pulling ability. (AA)

Fruehauf introduced stainless steel trailers to the trucking industry in 1940. This one is being towed by a 2-1/2-ton 1940 Reo Model 21B tractor. The six-wheel cab has 7.00 x 20 eight-ply Kelly-Springfield tires mounted. (AA)

Walker Vehicle Company, of Chicago, Illinois, still made delivery trucks in 1940. This one worked for United Parcel Service in New York. Walker offered seven electric and five gas-electric models, the latter available in low-aisle frame and straight-frame versions with or without standard bodies. (AA)

"Refresh yourself, drink Coca-Cola," it says on this 1941 Chevy 1-1/2-ton COE bottle truck. Chevy offered a total of 10 trucks of this style and capacity. Four models were offered with a choice of two wheelbases (109-3/8 or 132-5/3 inches) and two had a 158-1/8-inch stance. Prices were $719 to $968. (AA)

This 158-inch wheelbase 1941 Ford cab-over-engine bottle truck is either a Model 118W (85 horsepower) or Model 198W (90 horsepower). Both had a 15,600 pound GVW rating and varied only in engine output. The chassis price for the first was $920, while the latter cost $26 more. (AA)

Here's another long wheelbase 1941 Ford COE beverage truck. This one has a refrigerated, van-type body with a decorative roof rail and rear fender skirts. A new option for 134-inch and 158-inch COEs was a reinforced frame. Note the price of 5-cents for the "bigger-better" bottle of Pepsi! (AA)

A pretty streamliner that still put in a hard day's work was this 1941 GMC cab-over-engine Texaco tank truck. It has twin skirted rear fenders shielding the tandem dual rear wheels! (AA)

New for 1941 was the GMC Model AY COE truck. This is a 3-1/2-ton AY-700-701 with the 120-inch wheelbase. This truck used a 4-1/8 x 4-1/2 six-cylinder engine with 40.8 SAE horsepower and had 10-ply 8.25 x 20 tires front and rear. Chassis price was $4,990. The streamlined Richfield tanker body was extra.

Hudson Motor Car Company of Detroit, Michigan introduced the Model C-10 All-Purpose delivery van in its 1941 truck line up. It was a 1/2-ton model riding a 116-inch wheelbase with 6.00 x 16 tires. The 3 x 4-1/8-inch six developed 92 horsepower at 4000 rpm. It weighed 3,120 pounds and cost $1,176. (OCW)

This was the army truck to have working for you if you had to get your tank from point A to point B. In 1941, Mack introduced the LF and LJ heavy-duty trucks; LFT and LJT tractors; and LF and LH six-wheelers. Mack Thermodyne gas engines or Mack Lanowa diesel engines were offered in all models. (GTR)

This 1941 Studebaker Model M15 refrigerated van took Bonnie Doon ice cream products to customers in Mishawaka and South Bend, Indiana. It's a 1-1/2-ton, probably with the middle (126-inch) wheelbase. The engine was a six with 3 x 4 inch bore and stroke and 80 horsepower. The chassis and cab was $765. (AA)

Coca-Cola in bottles was shipped in a 1941 Studebaker Model M16. This looks like the middle (152-inch) wheelbase version, which sold for $820 in chassis and cab format. The insulated cargo body was extra. M16s had the larger 3-5/16 x 4-3/8-inch 94 horsepower six. Dual rear wheels were a $45 option. (AA)

Harry Short, of Ohio, employed a 1941 Studebaker Model M-16 in his horse racing stable business. The M-16 had a 1-1/2-ton rating. Up front were 6.00 x 20 six-ply tires, while 32 x 6 eight-ply tires were on the rear. (AA)

On May 27, 1941, President Franklin D. Roosevelt declared a state of national emergency and the first of $5 billion worth of war material orders were placed with America's automakers. Studebaker produced U.S. Army cargo trucks. (AA)

Owned by an Iowa truck collector, this 1942 GMC cab-over-engine platform truck showed up at an American Truck Historical Society meet. In 1942, the War Production Board identified five classes of users who could buy new civilian trucks, but approved only 640 of 33,000 purchasing applications. (OCW)

Response to war goods manufacturing was so strong, that nearly all wartime military vehicle production was completed by 1943. About 699,689 trucks and buses were built that year. Then, in 1944, civilian truck output rose to 737,524 units. This 1944 Mack EH was one of them. The chassis sold for $2,170.

The Automotive Council for War Production was dissolved in October 1945 and truck makers built 655,683 civilian models that year. This is a civilian-style 1945 GMC stake rack truck that was purchased by the United States Navy. Did that make it a civilian or military production unit? (GMC)

By the mid-1930s, Railway Express Agency was one of the nation's largest truck users with a fleet of 9,036 on America's roads. This is a 1946 Ford REA delivery truck. (OCW)

"Mr. Ed" couldn't stop talking about his good-looking 1948 GMC cab-over-engine van. The highly streamlined horse truck had a gross vehicle weight of 13,150 pounds and 8.25 x 20 tires. (GMC)

Spangler Duals were heavy-duty four-axle trucks with steering on both front axles. They were made from 1947 to 1949 by D.H. Spangler Engineering and Sales Company of Hamburg, Pennsylvania. Each rear axle was separately driven by a 100 horsepower Ford V-8. This stake truck has a 1947 license plate. (NAHC)

This 1947 Ford fire truck belongs to Rawhide Ranch in New London, Wisconsin. Rawhide accepts tax-deductible vehicle donations for its young residents to refurbish and sell for the benefit of the youth home. It is operated by former Green Bay Packer player and coach Bart Starr. (OCW)

The Coca-Cola distributor in San Antonio, Texas ordered this streamlined late-1947 GMC bottle truck. It sports General Motor's all-new postwar "Advance-Design" styling, which was to survive through early 1955. (AA)

Two-tone finish highlights the cab of this 1947 Studebaker M-16 1-1/2-ton single-compartment tank truck. Like many other truck manufacturers, Studebaker produced early postwar trucks that looked identical to prewar models. (AA)

William Mills Coal Company was lucky to find this GMC cab-over-engine dump truck for sale during the postwar shortage of new vehicles. The 1948 license plates indicate its vintage. The chrome-plated deluxe grille is unusual. (AA)

Brink's commissioned International-Harvester to built this custom-designed armored car on a 1948 International truck chassis. The rear "watch tower" style gun turret gave the armed guard an especially good view of his surroundings. A record of 1,349,582 trucks and buses were made in 1948. (BAC)

The Fargo name was used on the Dodge truck clones marketed in Canada from 1928-1972. These trucks were actually manufactured at Dodge Main, in Warren, Michigan. After 1972, the Fargo was discontinued in Canada, though the trucks continued selling in Africa, the Middle East, Scandinavia and elsewhere.

Last year for Studebaker's M16 was 1948. The 1-1/2-ton truck came with 128-inch, 152-inch and 195-inch wheelbases. This looks like the 128-inch, which had a chassis and cab price of $1,424. The GVW for all M16s was 13,500 pounds. They had 7.00 x 20 tires on the single front and dual rear wheels. (AA)

Pfeifer Coal Company, located on Diversey Avenue, used a new Autocar Model U50T COE truck to make deliveries when this photo was taken January 1, 1949. It had a 4 x 5 inch six with 119 horsepower at 2800 rpm. The chassis sold for $5,940. This one features the optional 112-inch wheelbase. (OCW)

Livestock Transport Company used a 1949 Chevrolet Model SV Series 6100 stake to ship cattle. A 93 horsepower six with 3-9/16 x 3-15/16 bore and stroke was used in this 5,255 pound truck. This 2-ton model was rated for 15,000 pounds GVW and sold for $1,966. Tires were 7.50 x 20 front and (dual) rear. (AA)

North American Freight Lines used a Series 6100 Model 6103 Chevrolet 2-ton tractor to haul this short, stainless steel Fruehauf trailer. This series featured a 137-inch wheelbase. The chassis and cab retailed for $1,759 and tipped the scales at 4,405 pounds. (AA)

Employed by the Bell Telephone Company of Pennsylvania was a 1949 Diamond T utility cabinet truck. Material shortages and strikes held truck output to 1,160,568 units this year. (AA)

Freightliner introduced its first Model 900 sleeper cab truck in 1949, but this is WF 800 cab-over-engine model. This brand was launched in 1940 when Leland James, president of Consolidated Freightways of Salt Lake City, grew dissatisfied with trucks on the market in the late 1930s and made his own.

In New York City, the Bureau of Highways in the Borough of Queens bought a shiny new 1949 GMC heavy-duty dump truck. This year, GMC's range of conventional dumps ran from 150- to 190 horsepower and 165-inch to 201-inch wheelbases with prices from $7,400 to $11,260 (AA)

Bringing Coca-Cola in bottles to customers in California is a 1948 International Model KB-5 bottle truck. This was a 1-1/2-ton series powered by a 3-5/16 x 4-1/2-inch six generating 93 horsepower at 3400 rpm. Factory list for the mid-size 159-inch chassis and cab was $1,678. Bodies were extra. (AA)

The 1949 Studebaker 16A and 17A models offered Adjusto-Air seat cushions that could be adjusted to the weight of the driver. "Fresh up with 7-Up," it says on the side of this 1949 Studebaker bottle truck at work for an Ohio beverage distributor. Note the new "bombsight" hood ornament. (AA)

Cy's Country Store sold Pillsbury's Best Feeds, which were delivered on a 1950 Chevrolet 4100 Series plat-form and stake truck. This 1-1/2-ton model came standard with a 137-inch wheelbase and dual rear wheels. (CMD)

Chevrolet also offered the Series 4400 long wheelbase 1-1/2-ton express platform and stake truck in 1950. It had a two-foot longer wheelbase than the 4100, but used the same 3-9/16 x 3-15/16-inch overhead valve six. This one was owned by the Riverside City Schools, which used it to haul gravel. (CMD)

"Nation's Leader in Value," was the sales slogan used on billboards advertising Chevrolet's 1950 line of heavy-duty trucks. Artist Richard Jemison designed this billboard for Campbell-Ewald Company. (OAI)

W.R. Koenig distributed Saratoga sandwich meats with a 1950 Diamond T Model 322 van. This was the truck maker's smallest 1-1/2-ton series using the same 3-7/16 x 4-1/4-inch, 91 horsepower six employed in 1-tons. Riding a 127-inch wheelbase, the 322 had a 12,000 pound GVW. It had size 6.00 x 17 tires. (AA)

A 1950 Diamond T Model 420 bottle truck carries 7-Up to thirsty consumers. This 1-1/2-ton model used a 3-5/8 x 4-1/4-inch six that developed 94 horsepower at 3000 rpm. It had a 130-inch wheelbase, a chassis weight of 5,800 pounds and a 16,300 pound GVW. The chassis and cab cost $2,340. (Bryce Morris)

Here's a 1950 Diamond T Model 420 with a special stake style cargo body featuring skirted rear fenders. It was operated by the Diamond T Motor Car Company's sales and service branch in Chicago, Illinois. The 420s had 6.00 x 20 six-ply tires all around, with dual rears as standard equipment. (AA)

Trucks in Diamond T's 620 series (here's a 1950 Model 622 stake) were rated at 2-1/2-tons and a 21,200 pound GVW. They had a 130-inch wheelbase and big 7.50 x 20 tires. The chassis and cab weighed 7,000 pounds and cost $3,480. Under the hood was a 4 x 4-1/4-inch six with 113 horsepower at 3000 rpm. (AA)

Parked outside a Borden Hostess House Restaurant is a 1950 Diamond T tractor and tank trailer truck operated by the Borden Company. During that year, the National Highway Users reported that 57 percent of all trucks in service were used for hauling food and dairy products.

A 1950 Ford F-7 hauled goods for the H.N. Lund Coal Company of Chicago. This was a 2-1/2-ton series using the 145 horsepower flathead V-8. Wheelbases of 135 to 195 inches were offered and they had a GVW of 19,000 pounds. The price range from the smallest ($3,058) to largest ($6,058) chassis and cab was wide.

This fleet of 1950 GMC Model FC-351s was owned by Pacific Coal & Supply Company of Cleveland, Ohio. The trucks had coal bodies made by Gar Wood Industries. The FC-351 had a 137-inch wheelbase, 7.50 x 20 tires and 16,000 pound GVW. The chassis & cab weighed 4,800 pounds and cost $1,775. (GMC)

A 1950 GMC Model FF-351 was used by D.E. Duffey & Sons in Philadelphia, Pennsylvania. It was equipped with a Hi-Lift Dump body built by Cresci to haul coal. This COE had a 122-inch wheelbase, 7.50 x 20 tires and 16,000 pound GVW. The chassis & cab weighed 4,540 pounds and cost $1,905. (GMC)

Workers for a Raleigh, North Carolina Coca-Cola distributor pile a load of bottle crates onto a 1950 International L-150 beverage delivery truck. Note the "gull-wing" body panels. The L-150 was a 1- to 1-1/2-ton series with a 130-inch wheelbase and a basic chassis and cab price of just $1,527. (AA)

An employee of a California bottler loads his hand truck with Coca-Cola crates removed from a 1950 International bottle truck. This L-160 COE was in a 3/4-ton to 1-1/2-ton series with a 3-9/16 x 3-11/16-inch of 30.4 SAE horsepower. With a 130-inch wheelbase, it had a chassis price of $1,911. (AA)

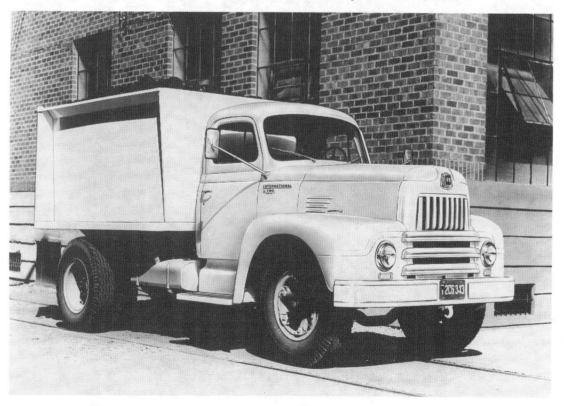

Despite a strike, material shortages and the start of fighting in Korea, the year 1950 saw production of 1,377,261 new trucks and buses. International's new L Series bowed that season. This is the L-190 diesel-powered dump truck.

Sporting an eye-catching red and white paint scheme, this 1950 Seagrave 1000-gallon pumper was used by the Winterhaven, Florida Fire Department into at least the mid-1970s. Truck historian Elliott Kahn snapped the photo in October, 1974.

The 1950 Mercury truck was a Canadian clone of the contemporary domestic Ford model. This 1-1/2-ton stake-bodied model showed up at an antique truck meet. The Mercury grille had only four bars, compared to five on the Ford. They were built on the the same assembly line as Fords manufactured in Windsor, Ontario.

In 1950, the latest word in modern transportation for the brewery industry was the White 3000 with its high load capacity, low energy-saving cab and short wheelbase. This one delivered Pabst Blue Ribbon beer. (AA)

Hard at work for the Handley Lumber Company of Orlando, Florida is a 1951 Diamond T Model 322 stake truck. Total production of commercial vehicles in the United States actually climbed to 1,450,596 units this year. (AA)

Pictured near the White House in 1951 is a new Diamond T Model 420 wrecker with license plates indicating that it worked for the District of Columbia Police Department. It was ready to enforce the "No Parking This Side" rule that the street sign behind the truck indicated. (AA)

Montgomery Herefords were transported to market in a livestock trailer towed by a 1951 Diamond T Model 660 tractor with an outside sun visor. The 660 was a gasoline-engine model. It had a 162 horsepower six-cylinder motor. (AA)

A 1951 Diamond T cab over engine tractor delivers a load of Dutch Boy Paint dockside. Perhaps the ship in the background, named the Hawaiian Fisherman, was being repainted. The stake-style trailer, like those used for shipping livestock, must have helped alleviate the smell of paint solvents. (AA)

Jaeger Sand and Gravel Company of Wisconsin used a 1951 Diamond T Model 723 diesel tractor to pull a Fruehauf trailer. This combination had a GVW of 33,500 pounds. Despite high sales of postwar models like this one, 33 percent of the trucks on America's highways in 1951 were still pre-1940 editions. (AA)

With a list price of $1,895, the middle wheelbase (158 inches) Ford F-5 stake was a bargain in the 1-1/2-ton truck field in 1951. Its standard features included the 3.19 x 3.75-inch, 32.5 SAE horsepower Ford V-8 and dual rear wheels. It tipped the scales at 5,145 pounds and had a 14,000 pound GVW. (AA)

Bottlers reported that the 1951 White 3000 was ideal for their business because its low cab speeded driver movements and its short wheelbase assured maximum maneuverability. This one was owned by the Atlanta Coca-Cola Bottling Company. (AA)

The Broadview Fire Department used this 1952 American LaFrance Model 700 pumper. This cab-forward series of fire trucks was announced in 1945 and put into production in 1947. The was as exclusive offering from the Elmira, New York Company until 1956. (OCW)

Central Distributing Company of Charleston, West Virginia hauled Carling's Red Cap Ale and Black Label Beer in an insulated van constructed on a 1952 Diamond T Model 422 chassis. (AA)

Etna Concrete Block Company operated this ready mixed concrete truck with a Jaeger Transit truck mixer mounted on a 1952 Diamond T Model 720 chassis. This type of mixer was of a postwar design patented in both the United States and foreign countries. (AA)

Pittsburgh Wholesale Distributing Company hauled this handsomely-trimmed Fruehauf trailer with a 1952 Diamond T Model 620 tractor. The 620 series carried a 2-1/2-ton rating and used a 4-5/16 x 4-7/8-inch six-cylinder gasoline engine which put out 143 horsepower at 2600 rpm. (AA)

This stainless steel Dorsey trailer was insulated to protect the perishables shipped by L.A. Keegstra Produce Company of Grand Rapids, Michigan. It was hauled with a 1952 Diamond T Model 572 tractor with a sleeper cab. This tractor-trailer weighed 9,320 pounds and used size 10.00 x 20 tires. (AA)

Schield's & Son of Norwood Park, Illinois employed a 1952 Diamond T Model 622 dump truck in its construction business. This heavy-duty gas-engined truck had a 14,600 pound GVW. (AA)

This trailer used for long-distance transportation of household goods was owned by Cary Transport, of Eau Claire, Wisconsin. This company was an agent for Indianapolis, Indiana-based Clipper Van Lines. The Fruehauf trailer was pulled by a 1952 Diamond T Model 720 tractor. (AA)

White Cross Sleep Products of Philadelphia, Pennsylvania shipped mattresses, sofa beds, sleeper sofas and studio couches in a 1952 Diamond T Model 420 with a furniture body that extended over the cab. According to a sign on the side, White Cross mattresses featured "Even-ized" innerspring construction. (AA)

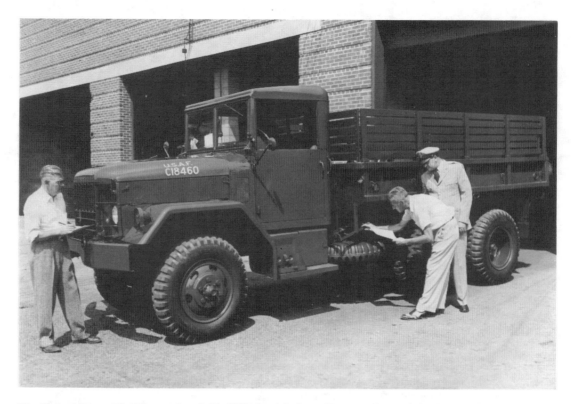

The United States Air Force ordered this 1952 Studebaker military stake truck for Korean War service. The conflict overseas continued to impact the industry with material shortages and threats of shutting down steel furnaces. Production of trucks and buses dropped to 1,238,193 units. (OCW)

This Freightliner Model WF-8164 cab-over-engine truck may have been used for mounting dozens of different purpose-built bodies. (WTD)

Hard at work for a fictitious company named McLott Ore Handlers is a 1953 Chevrolet Series 6400 dump truck. The 6400 line offered a range of 1-1/2-ton trucks with chassis and cab prices starting at $2,068. A 161-inch wheelbase and dual rear wheels were featured on these heavy-duty models. (CMD)

Pearl Brewing Company of San Antonio, Texas produced the "Gem of Fine Beers" and shipped it in a gem of a truck. The 1953 Diamond T Model 420C had a special Bedell beverage delivery body highlighted by fully enclosed rear wheels. Bedell Body Company was also located in San Antonio. (AA)

C.A. Tilt, chairman of the board, must have felt like this Diamond T Tilt-Cab Tractor was named for him. He founded the Chicago company to make automobiles in 1905 and expanded into trucks six years later. This new-for-1953 model had a cab that tilted forward for servicing without need of power unit. (DTM)

Diamond T's cab-over-engine model was well-suited to sanitation service. This one sports a Leach garbage disposal truck body. Most Diamond Ts (53 percent) were trucks in the above-26,000 pounds GVW class. (AA)

This 1953 Diamond T Model 323 worked for George S. Daugherty Company, of Pittsburgh, distributing quality canned foods. The production of 8,059 Diamond Ts this year was the highest since 1948, when 12,684 had been built. It would have been even higher, except for a strike and vendor disputes. (AA)

An employee of Jewel Food Stores' Lemont, Illinois supermarket is hand-trucking a load of perishables delivered by a 1953 Diamond T cab-over-engine cargo van. Operated by James A. Hannah, Incorporated, the truck had a 10,680 pound EW. "A Better Place to Trade" was the Jewel motto. (AA)

George Kaiser, of Glenolden, Pennsylvania brought this restored 1953 Ford F-500 wrecker to the Antique Automobile Club of America Fall National Meet at Hershey, Pennsylvania in October, 1990. The F-500 was a 1-1/2-ton model offered with a choice of 130- or 154-inch wheelbases. (OCW)

Norwalk Truck Line used this van. It was one of 31,596 Studebaker trucks made in 1953, including the last of 38,029 military 2-1/2-ton units on a government contract. The base 2R15 model was a 1-ton with a 10,000 pound GVW. Door markings and dual rear wheels indicate this one was set up for heavier loads.

Dual rear wheels were optional on 1954 Chevrolet 1-ton, Series 3800 conventional trucks. The platform and stake model had a 137-inch wheelbase and a base price of $1,794. It tipped the scales at 4,200 pounds. Note the all-new one-piece curved windshield. (CMD)

A new cross-bar grille was seen on 1954 Chevrolet trucks. Here's a pair of 161-inch wheelbase 6400 Series 2-ton dumps at work for Cahill Excavating Company. The chassis and cab sold for $2,067. That included an overhead valve six, dual rear wheels and four-speed manual transmission. (CMD)

Owned by a member of the American Truck Historical Society, this 1955 International COE tractor was exhibited at a Model T show in Cross Plains, Wisconsin. IHC produced 121,522 trucks in 1953 and 11,470 of them were truck tractors. A 1950 Fruehauf trailer is being pulled by this classic. (OCW)

A total of only 3,568 trucks were assembled by Diamond T Motor Car Company for 1955. New was a "low-floor" drop-frame series. This Model 422 cargo van employed at DiGirolamo Produce Company in Bracken-ridge, Pennsylvania was a carryover model. Diamond T also assembled Internationals under agreement. (AA)

In Clairton, Pennsylvania, the local agent for United Van Lines used a 1954 Diamond T Tilt-Cab COE tractor to haul a drop-frame trailer during household moves. This combination weighed 9,300 pounds and used 9.00 x 20 tires. (AA)

Fred Sykes, a 25-year member of the Eagle Rescue Squad in Little Falls, New Jersey, sent this photo of the Little Falls Fire Department's 1954 Ford "Big Job" Model 106 rescue truck. It appears to be a C-700 3-ton cab-over-engine model on a 144-inch wheelbase. This truck had a chassis and cab price of $4,764.

A tower reflected in the door indicates this 1954 Studebaker eight-foot stake truck was used by forest rangers. The base 3R11 was a 3/4-ton with single rear wheels, but this one has a heavy-duty chassis package. It cost just under $2,000. Studebaker built 182 trucks with automatic transmissions in 1954. (AA)

Among the 15,236 trucks built by Studebaker in 1954 was this 2-1/2-ton military model. On June 22, 1954, Studebaker-Packard Corporation announced a consolidation subject to stockholder approval. On August 17, the merger of the two firms was completed and approved. (AA)

In 1955, Diamond T produced 5,180 trucks, an increase of 45 percent over the previous year. The sales of Tilt-Cab models was greatly expanded, particularly in the area of highway tractors like this one parked near a United States Steel Company facility. It was operated by Enterprise Transfer Company of Chicago, Illinois.

Hines-Colby Company used this 1955 Ford F-500 "Big Job" dump at a construction site. The badge on the grille indicates that it has a 3.5 x 3.1-inch bore and stroke, 239 cubic-inch overhead valve V-8. Ford built a record 373,897 trucks in 1955 and sales of its biggest models rose 34.8 percent. (AA)

Oshkosh Truck Company built just 300 trucks in 1955, so this is a rare vehicle parked outside Nesbitt Equipment Company. It has a Rex "Adjusta-Wate" moto-mixer mounted at the rear of the heavy-duty, all-wheel drive chassis. Oshkosh Motor Truck Corporation's home is in Oshkosh, Wisconsin. (OTC)

Two workman load freight from a Missouri Pacific Lines railcar onto a 1955 Studebaker E-28 stake. This 1-1/2-ton line included 9-foot (131-inch wheelbase); 12-foot (155-inch wheelbase); and 14-foot (171-inch wheelbase) stake models. Prices ranged from $1,260 to $1,365. This truck has a V-8. (AA)

The Dorseyville Fire Department owned this 1956 Diamond T Model 620 fire truck with Howe body work. Diamond T made 5,061 trucks of all types in 1956 and had net sales of $45.4 million. During the year, a division was formed to manufacture parts previously purchased from outside vendors. (AA)

Thompson Flying Service used this 1956 Diamond T tank truck to transport aviation gas at its approved aircraft repair station in Salt Lake City, Utah. The truck-maker had a net income of $1,293,320 that year. More than 79 percent of its vehicles were heavy-duty models, compared to 60 percent in 1955. (OCW)

Tex Crete Concrete Building Products Company of Texas was another Diamond T customer. The company's Model 520 flat bed had a special hoisting mechanism to lift Kaydite block and Holiday Hill stone onto the back of the truck. (AA)

In Berwyn, Pennsylvania the Berwyn Lumber Company used a 1956 Diamond T cab-over-engine truck with an hydraulic hoist to stack big loads of long boards and heavy lumber. Though Diamond T output declined, its new concentration on heavier, specialty models compensated for the lost business. (AA)

A driver for Collins Concrete Company, of Keansburg, New Jersey, visits the gravel pit with a 1957 Diamond T Model 9205W. It carries a Rex engine-powered transit mixer requiring its own fuel tank behind the roof of the cab. E.J. Rush became board chairman of Diamond T, replacing founder C.A. Tilt. (AA)

The City of Vermillion Fire Department had a 1957 Ford C-Series Tilt-Cab tanker with Custom Cab equipment. Ford marked its 40th consecutive year of mass-producing trucks during 1957. During the year, all heavy-duty truck manufacturing operations were transferred to the Louisville, Kentucky plant.

Truck collector Francis Walsh of Messena, New York takes his 1957 Mack H-63 cab-over-engine tractor to Antique Truck Club of America shows. Mack saw production of 17,360 units and set a sales record of $263,660,325. Net earnings were $11,072,820. It owned Brockway and C.D. Beck Company. (ATC)

Two-tone paint schemes were a hot selling-feature at Studebaker in 1957, but this 1-1/2-ton Transtar stake truck was not a hot seller. In fact, the company's commercial vehicle output dropped to just 9,374 or one percent of industry. A special truck equipment directory was sent to its dealer network.

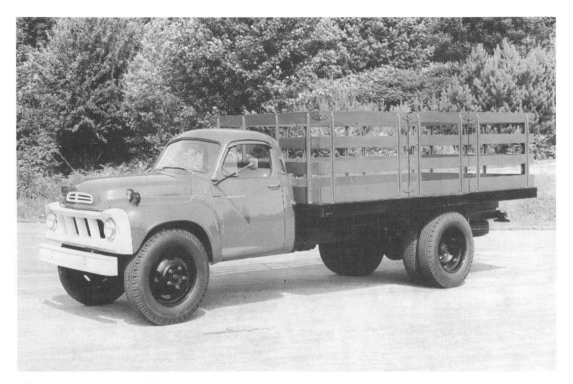

One of the largest Studebaker products available in 1957 was this Transtar 2-ton heavy-duty Model 3E40B with a 171-inch wheelbase and 14-foot stake body. It had a factory advertised price of $3,325 and weighed 6,260 pounds with a 19,000 pound GVW. Under the hood was a 289 cubic-inch Torque Star HD V-8. (AA)

Employed by Patterson Supply Company was a 1958 Diamond T Model 830 with a Smith redi-mixer. This was an historic year. Effective April 1, 1958, White Motor Company purchased Diamond T's inventories, patents, trade-name and goodwill for about $10,100,000 in cash and it became the DTM Corporation. (AA)

Typical of the diversified line of Dodge trucks for 1958 were these models: (left to right) D100 pickup; D100 Town Wagon; D300 stake; D100 Town Panel; and T700 six-wheeler with trailer. The company claimed its products satisfied 98 per cent of all hauling needs. (DTD)

Fender skirts dressed up this 1958 Ford F-Series Cab bottle truck. Truck production by the Ford Division during 1958 totaled 242,890. This represented 27.8 percent market share, compared to 31.1 percent in 1957. However, Ford was the clear king in the 16,000 to 19,500 pound class with 52,950 units. (AA)

GMC Truck & Coach Division of General Motors turned out 61,768 trucks in 1958. They included this Model T1546 "Turbopowered" tractor attached to a long tank trailer. A new model was the lightweight DR 862 highway tractor that tipped the scales at just 11,000 pounds with 100 gallons of fuel. (AA)

Truck collector Jack Muller, of Dalton, Pennsylvania brings his 1958 Mack Model TK tractor to Antique Truck Club of America shows. Mack turned out a total of 14,606 trucks, including 1,067 by Brockway. However, it was the nation's number one producer of diesel-engined trucks with 10,018 built. (ATC)

Hillyard Floor Treatments Company of St. Joseph, Missouri pulled this handsome Trailmobile trailer with a 1959 Diamond T conventional diesel tractor. Nine transmissions, eleven rear axles and five diesel engines were available for the 6,017 Diamond Ts made that calendar year. (AA)

New technology was evidenced by the snorkel mounted on this 1959 Ford cabinet body truck owned by the Service First Utility Equipment Company. The snorkel is manufactured by Pitman. (OCW)

Introduced in November 1958, the 1959 Studebaker line of trucks ran from 1/2-ton Scotsman models with a six-cylinder engine to 2-ton Transtar series trucks with GVWs up to 19,000 pounds. This is the 4E30 2-ton with dual rear wheels and a 9-foot stake body. (AA)

This 1959 White 5464 diesel tractor pulled tandem trailers for Spector Freight Systems, Incorporated of Chicago, Illinois. The Cleveland, Ohio truck-maker's product line now included White and Reo trucks 16,000 pounds GVW and up; Autocar trucks 26,000 pounds and up; White school buses and Diamond T trucks.

In 1960, Chevrolet truck production reached 394,014, the highest total in nine years. This C-80 diesel worked for the Pennsylvania Railroad. Chevrolet built 58,138 trucks in the 16,001 to 19,500 pound GVW class and 8,586 in the 19,501 to 26,000 pound GVW range, but only 778 with GVWs over 26,001 pounds. (CMD)

The Howe Fire Apparatus Company of Anderson, Indiana was established in 1872 and built its first pumper on a motorized chassis in 1907. Beginning in 1932, the company began building its own fire trucks. These 1960 Howe pumpers served the volunteer fire departments in Hampton Township and West Elizabeth. (Howe)

D.J. Potter Company delivered fuel oil to customers in Laureldale, Pennsylvania with this cab-over-engine tanker. It was one of only 2,468 Diamond T trucks built during 1960. A new series of Tilt-Cabs with fiberglass cabs was introduced, along with a line of "West Coast" diesel models. (AA)

This 1960 GMC Crew Cab pickup was used by the Erie Lakawana Railroad as a track service vehicle. It was modified so that it could be operated both on rails or on pavement. It had the V-6 power plant that GMC introduced that season, which was very popular with truck buyers. (GMC)

The Indian River Volunteer Fire Department operated this 1960 GMC Model A6011 Seagrave tanker. It had a V-6 engine. GMC was America's fifth largest truck maker that year, with 100,521 units built. A 33.3 percent sales increase was the largest in the industry and attributed to the new V-6. (GMC)

Outfitted for fire department rescue service, this 1960 GMC cab-over-engine truck has the Tilt-Cab. C.J. Werner was general manager of GMC Truck & Coach Division, of Pontiac, Michigan, in 1960. In addition to building over 100,000 trucks, the company produced 3,806 motor coaches. (OCW)

GMC's 1960 Model P2503 1-ton stake truck had a 133-inch wheelbase. It sold for $2,529 and weighed 4,810 pounds. The 305-A overhead valve V-6 had a 4.25 x 3.58-inch bore and stroke and displaced 304.7 cubic inches. This engine produced 150 horsepower at 3600 rpm and 260 pounds-feet of torque at 1600 rpm.

Clarence Little, of Hummelstown, Pennsylvania is the owner of this 1960 Mack Model B61 tractor. Mack manufactured 14,438 units that year. The company employed about 11,000 people at three plants in Allentown, Pennsylvania, Plainfield, New Jersey and Cortland, New York. (ATHS)

FWD built 939 trucks in 1961, an increase of 167 from the previous year. The firm's specialty was heavy-duty models with 17,000 to 60,000 pound GVWs including vehicles designed for use in oil fields, road maintenance and utility work. This hoist truck was built for the New York Central Railroad.

In 1961, Studebaker built 7,648 trucks, the fewest in a decade. A 130 horsepower General Motors Detroit Diesel engine was planned for 1962 introduction, but a few diesels were built as early as June 1961 for testing. The grille and door lettering on this 1961 tractor indicate its engine type.

Studebaker offered trucks with 16,000 to 23,000 pound GVWS and 131-inch to 195-inch wheelbases in 1961. Here's a heavy-duty 2-ton Transtar model with a long wheelbase and 14 foot stake body. It has the mid-1961 diesel engine option. The diesel was a four-cylinder, two-cycle power plant. (OCW)

229

A city collector working for the United States Post Office gets ready to transfer a sack of letters to his 1962 Postal Jeep. Willys-Jeep (soon to be renamed Kaiser-Jeep Corporation) earned government contracts worth more than $100 million in 1962. (KJC)

This four-wheel drive diesel powered dump truck was built by Duplex Truck Corporation in 1963. It was among an order for units built to carry an underbody scraper and V-blade snowplow. A total of 338 trucks were made by this Lansing, Michigan firm in 1963. (WSC)

Well-suited for bringing milk to households in Canada and other foreign markets, the 1963 Fargo P200/P300 stand-up delivery van was a clone of the Dodge version sold in the United States. It had dual rear wheels. (RPZ)

Military contracts boosted Studebaker's 1963 truck production to 13,119. This Model 8E40 Transtar stake bed was sold to the U.S. Marine Corps by the firm's Defense Products Division. $75,000 in military research money was awarded to develop an advanced design 8 x 8 heavy-duty truck and a 1/8-ton cargo carrier.

Euclid was a Cleveland, Ohio branch of General Motors from 1953 until anti-trust regulations prompted its 1968 sale to White. This is a 1964 Euclid 27-ton dump truck. The company built trucks as big as a 120-ton dump trailer with twin Cummins diesels generating 750 total horsepower and costing $170,000.

The Fargo name was used on Dodge clones as big as this 1964 PL-1000 Tilt-Cab diesel. Fargo Motor Corporation started as Chrysler's fleet sales division from 1928-1932. Then, it technically became a part of Dodge Division. Some Dodge trucks produced in Britain and Australia also used the Fargo name. (RPZ)

Sales of "Jeep" vehicles set an all-time record for Kaiser-Jeep Corporation in 1964. Helping to achieve 120,830 production units was an order from the United States Post Office, which ordered 3,868 "Fleetvan" delivery trucks. These were nick-named "Zip-Vans" to promote Zip Code use by mailers. (KJC)

Dodge's huge 1965 heavy-duty NL-1000 Tilt-Cab diesel was designed for over-the-road hauling. Its short COE configuration permitted longer trailer lengths to operate under existing regulations. Interstate Motor Freight System of Grand Rapids, Michigan pulled a Highway brand trailer with this one. (DTD)

Pulling a trailer made by Strick is a an R Series 6 x 4 tractor made by Mack. It illustrates one of the two new series (the other was called the U Series) added in 1965. The truck was one of 13,127 new Macks registered in that year. Diesel engines were installed in about 93 percent of those vehicles. (MTC)

The 1965 Dodge D-500 with Ashton service truck body was one of many specialty vehicles offered by Dodge. The heavy-duty model has a 15,000 pound, two-speed rear axle and optional dual rear wheels. It worked for Stan's Service, which was located somewhere in Michigan, according to the 1964 license plates. (DTD)

Warren A. Empey of Lexington, Massachusetts owns this 1966 Dodge Model WM300 Power Wagon with dump body. Dodge Truck produced 153,159 units in 1966, setting a record for peacetime output. The company's Warren, Michigan truck plant received a 140,000 square-foot expansion to keep up with booming sales.

The volunteer fire department in Lutz, Florida had this 1966 White Model 7000 tractor in its fleet when Elliott Kahn snapped this photo in August of 1974. It was perfect for pulling a tank-trailer loaded with water. White Trucks, a division of White Motor Corporation, turned out 32,422 trucks in 1966. (EK)

The versatile Universal Jeep could be useful in many applications. This 1966 CJ model was equipped as an in-plant utility vehicle. Kaiser-Jeep produced 99,624 vehicles this year. (KJC)

It looks like another vehicle struck this 1967 Ford N Series bottle truck that was owned by Peterson Stange Pepsi-Cola of Springfield, Missouri. During 1967, Ford Motor Company was also struck by the United Auto Workers union. This cost about 50,000 truck sales and held output down to 426,619 units. (OCW)

Freightliner Corporation reached an all-time production high of 8,672 White-Freightliner trucks in 1969. Only four of the trucks were built with gas engines; the rest were all diesels. This is the Model WFT-8164 COE tractor. A new 170,000 square-foot plant opened in Portland, Oregon this year. (WFC)

Modern Classics
1970-1994

No-lead fuels, air pollution, restraint systems and driver regulations were trucking concerns as the 1970s bowed. Production of trucks and buses in 1970 slid to 1,733,821. This Walter Airport Crash Truck was built for the Chicago Fire Department for use at O'Hare Airport. (WTC)

Rite-Way trucks were purpose-built concrete mixers made in Dallas, Texas, Fort Wayne, Indiana and Arlington, Texas starting in 1961. This 8 x 6 model, of 1971 vintage, was employed in construction projects undertaken by Keys Industries in Florida. Truck production leaped to 2,088,001 in 1971. (EK)

Commercial vehicle output climbed once again in 1972, hitting an all-time record of 2,482,503 trucks and buses. That year's Ford F600 is seen here in low rack stake format. It offered 180-inch, 186-inch and 212-inch wheelbases. A 300 cubic-inch six was standard on the 19,200 GVW heavy-duty truck. (FMC)

Special options like automatic transmission, fifth wheels, engine brakes, special seats and saddle fuel tanks were available for the 1972 Chevrolet HV70 line of 3- to 6-ton conventional diesels. The chassis and cab price for a rig like this one was $11,946 and it weighed about 8,270 pounds. (CMD)

The name on this rig ... Hajek ... brings to mind the fact that illegal truck hijackings cost American shippers over $1 billion during 1972. That's when this Hendrickson 6 x 4 COE tractor and Gindy trailer were used by Hajek Trucking Company of North Judson, Indiana, a highly respected firm. (OCW)

Now available in two-tone finish was the 1972 Chevrolet C-65. This was a 5-ton tractor with chassis and cab base priced at $5,413. It was offered with engines from a 379 cubic-inch V-6 to a 366 cubic-inch gas V-8. Size 8.25 x 20E tires were used and the GVW was 21,000 to 29,000 pounds. (CMD)

In 1973, Chevrolet offered the Turbine N-6 diesel on its new models with Cerametalix clutches and four- or five-speed Allison automatic transmissions. "Chevrolet: Building a better way to serve the USA" was the truck division's sales slogan that year. (CMD)

This 1973 International Loadstar 1800 6 x 4 truck with dump body has taken on a heavy load of gravel from the hoppers behind it at a stone quarry. Brooks McCormick, a descendant of Cyrus McCormick (who invented the reaping machine) was president and chief executive officer of International Harvester. (IHC)

In 1974, Chevrolet scored its second-best truck sales year in company history with calendar-year sales of 885,362 units. Production was an even higher 899,559 trucks of all sizes. This is a 1974 Step-Van King bucket truck with Telstar aerial lift conversion designed for one-man operation. (CMD)

Of the Chevrolet trucks made in calendar 1974, most (895,366) were gasoline powered and 4,193 used diesel engines. This gas-powered sanitation truck is hard at work cleaning up the environment. In Washington, D.C., Secretary of Transportation Brock Adams got after truck-makers to up fuel economy. (CMD)

Here's a Tilt-Cab Chevrolet sanitation truck picking up garbage from a restaurant. The gas-engine Tilt-Cabs came in T-60 (3-ton) and T-65 (4-1/2-ton) series with 133- or 175-inch wheelbases. A 350 cubic-inch V-8 was standard in the small series, while the large one came with at least 366 cubic inches.

Chevrolet's truck line included a 2- to 3-ton C-60 conventional, available with a large stake body. Midwest Body Incorporated, of Paris, Illinois, was a firm that specialized in building stake bodies. Base-priced at $4,903, the 1974 C-60 offered gas engines from a 292 cubic-inch six to 427 cubic-inch V-8. (CMD)

Leading manufacturers of van-type truck bodies in 1974 were Sheller-Globe Corporation; Wayne Corporation's Wayne Transportation Division and Wayne Corporation's Wells Corporation Limited subsidiary. This van body was mounted on a two-tone 1974 Chevrolet truck chassis. (CMD)

This 1974 Chevrolet 90 series conventional-cab truck with a diesel engine is hauling a heavy load of steel cable from a factory. Detroit and Cummins diesel power plants were available in Chevrolet trucks. They included two- and four-cycle motors with 11 ratings ranging from 201 to 300 SAE net horsepower. (CMD)

Distinctive styling characterized Chevrolet's Titan 90 Series truck line up. In addition to its two-tone finish, this Tilt-Cab Titan could be ordered with a two-zone heater to maintain comfortable temperatures for the driver inside. The sleeper section of the cab had its own heater. (CMD)

A 1974 Chevrolet Series 60 steel Tilt-Cab with semi-trailer designed for hauling beverage cases. Chevrolet's short 72-inch Tilt-Cab with set-back front axle gave better load balance and allowed longer trailer length. Rigs like this had 17,000-25,000 pound GVWs and chassis and cab prices from $6,618. (CMD)

Total commercial vehicle production of all United States manufacturers fell to 2,746,538 units in calendar-year 1974. This Chevrolet 90 Series conventional cab diesel tractor was one of them. It's hauling a "monster-sized" dump-bodied trailer with 24 tires. (CMD)

One of America's small builders of big trucks was the Sutphen Fire Equipment Company of Amlin, Ohio. Originally a maker of fire fighting equipment, it began building its own chassis in 1967. Here is a 1974 Sutphen serial tower fire engine used by the Boca Raton Fire Department in Florida. (EK)

In 1974, International Harvester built 194,580 trucks in its North American factories. New for the year was a V-800 diesel and forged aluminum front axle. Work on federal "Quiet Truck" and anti-skid air brake regulations continued. This is a Transtar 4200 6 x 4 tractor and 3-axle trailer. (IHC)

The Nagle-Hart company used Oshkosh trucks to transport heavy equipment between its Madison, Milwaukee and Eau Claire, Wisconsin facilities. This 1974 E Series COE is hauling a Caterpillar tractor on a heavy-duty Hyster low-boy trailer. In the background are other Caterpillar road-building vehicles. (OTC)

A 1975 Caterpillar 777 dump truck was employed by the Taylor Woodrow Construction Company Limited, of Great Britain, for English construction products. With its load of 75 tons, the "Cat 777" was happy with all sorts of heavy-duty working conditions. (OMM)

A 1975 Chevrolet ME-65 tandem with dump body. Chevrolet's 1975 registrations by GVW included 523,638 trucks of 6,000 pounds or less; 237,451 of 6,001 to 10,000 pounds; 1,956 of 16,001 to 19,500 pounds; 36,617 of 19,501 to 26,000 pounds; 601 of 26,001 to 33,000 pounds; and 3,332 over 33,001 pounds. (CMD)

Chevrolet's 1975 Series CE65 Model CE66003 was the farm body version with a $7,041 base price. This 4-1/2-ton line offered wheelbases from 125- to 218-inches and GVWs of 21,200 to 34,000 pounds. Size 8.25 x 20E tires were standard equipment. Scottsdale cab trim was a $90 option. (CMD)

Like many trucks of its era, this 1975 Chevrolet CE65 was fitted with a tanker body. With the energy crunch and rapidly rising prices, the home fuel oil delivery business was prospering in the United States.

In trucking news this year was the mysterious disappearance of Teamster's Union boss Jimmy Hoffa. He vanished on July 20, 1975. Some members of Hoffa's organization operated 1975 Ford tractor trucks, such as the W9000 cab-over-engine (left) and L9000 conventional (right) linehaulers shown here. (FMC)

Production of White Freightliner trucks fell from 14,700 in 1974 to 4,891 in 1975, when this WFT-8164 conventional tractor was made. During the year, Consolidated Freightways announced that its exclusive distribution contract with White Motor Company (in effect since 1951) would end on March 8, 1976.

In 1975, International Harvester realized production of 118,241 trucks, a drop of 76,339 units from the prior year. The 1975 IHC semi-tractor and Fruehauf trailer seen in this photo dwarf the 1928 IHC truck that is parked beside them at the company's Fort Wayne, Indiana headquarters. (IHC)

Peterbilt registered approximately 5,000 new trucks in 1975, compared to 8,428 the previous season. A new cab-over-engine Model 352H was introduced that year. This 352 was photographed in Tampa, Florida by truck historian Elliott Kahn. There was also a new-for-1975 Model 387 heavy-duty truck.

Fairbanks International Airport in Alaska ordered this 1975 Walter 4 x 4 Model CBK airport crash truck for its emergency response team. Such trucks were originally developed working with the United States Government, the New York City Port Authority and the National Fire Protection Agency. (WMT)

The airport crash truck business was one segment of the market that seemed to be picking up in the mid-1970s, as air travel became more common. Here we see several Walters, and a smaller Dodge rescue vehicle, in readiness for emergencies near an airport terminal in 1975.

The Monessen Fire Department put this 1975 Ward LaFrance Ambassador pumper to work as Engine 18. This was a custom-bodied rig well-equipped for heavy-duty fire-fighting jobs. (WLF)

White Motor Corporation lost $53.8 million in 1975, when it built 13,311 trucks in the United States and 1,557 in Canada. Seen here is a 1975 White Constructor 6 x 4 dump truck at a construction site in Ohio. (WMC)

A 1976 Chevrolet C-60 delivery body truck. Chevrolet's 1976 registrations by GVW included 580,025 trucks of 6,000 pounds or less; 431,352 of 6,001 to 10,000 pounds; 1,926 of 16,001 to 19,500 pounds; 35,374 of 19,501 to 26,000 pounds; 633 of 26,001 to 33,000 pounds; and 3,128 over 33,001 pounds. (CMD)

Durability, ease of maintenance and driver comfort were items stressed in GMC's 1976 medium-duty models. Model year retail sales of big units rose to 2,492 motorhomes, 20,842 medium-duty trucks and 11,531 heavy-duty models. This compared to 1,315; 20,833; and 8,665, respectively, the previous year. (GMC)

Chevrolet offered the long-hooded Bison 115-inch BBC conventional with ample room under the hood for an 8V-71 Detroit diesel. Moving the engine forward permitted good engine accessibility and also provided more room inside the cab. Steel or aluminum frames were matched to loads by computer. (CMD)

For 1976, GMC's Astro 95 highway tractor could be ordered with a roof-mounted Dragfoiler and other components designed to increase fuel economy up to nine percent. In August, a new line of heavy-duty conventionals aimed directly at the owner-operator market dominated by independent producers bowed. (GMC)

A 1977 Chevrolet C-60 utility body truck. Chevrolet's 1977 registrations by GVW included 482,328 trucks of 6,000 pounds or less; 596,364 of 6,001 to 10,000 pounds; 1,795 of 16,001 to 19,500 pounds; 32,908 of 19,501 to 26,000 pounds; 1,031 of 26,001 to 33,000 pounds; and 2,997 over 33,001 pounds. (CMD)

An Omaha Standard livestock body on a 1977 Dodge D600. Dodge model year truck sales included 467,197, including some 5,000 in this medium-duty class. That compared to 406,654 total trucks and 9,591 medium-duty models in 1976. Production at the Warren, Michigan and St. Louis plants was a record 474,001.

A 1977 Euclid Euc R-35 dump truck gets another load of dirt from a "steam shovel." This truck used a 420 horsepower diesel to carry payloads up to 70,000 pounds. Euclid began 1977 as a division of White Motor Corporation, but was among several White interests sold to Mercedes-Benz during the year. (WMC)

Oshkosh Truck set a 1977 sales record, including 33 Class 8 diesel 4 x 4s and 258 Class 8 tandem-axle 6 x 6s. This J Series truck featured an 8V-71 Detroit Diesel and automatic transmission. Options were 250 to 450 horsepower engines and 9- to 10-speed manual and 4- to 8-speed automatic transmissions. (OTC)

Ready to ship out of snowy Wisconsin to Texas is this 1977 Oshkosh A Series Snorkel truck purchased by the Lubbock Fire Department. The A was a custom fire truck chassis available with single or tandem rear axles. It featured a 350 horsepower engine and four-speed automatic transmission. (OTC)

One reason Ford topped Chevrolet in 1978 sales was the introduction of the Class 8 CL9000 cab-over-engine truck in early October. Ford beat Chevrolet and GMC combined in medium- and heavy-duty truck sales this year. Its model year sales in these classes totaled 94,130 units, versus 81,459 in 1977. (FMC)

Another Wisconsin-based fire truck maker was Peter Pirsch & Sons Company, of Kenosha. This is their 1977 Senior Aerial Ladder truck in a format built for the Trenton New Jersey Fire Department.

Model year sales for 1978 GMCs included 27,600 medium-duty, 20,000 heavy-duty and 2,250 motorhomes. New was this heavy-duty short-nose conventional called the Brigadier. It had a durable and lightweight four-piece fiberglass front end, added driver comfort, more efficiency and bigger windshield. (GMC)

This custom 1978 Kenworth pickup was built for retiring company executive Murray Aiken, seen here with his beautiful retirement gift. During that year, Kenworth retailed 14,948 new trucks and earned fifth slot in the Class 8 truck sales race. Behind the pickup is a full-size Kenworth long-hood conventional. (TST)

The 1978 Oshkosh F Series all-wheel drive truck was for construction, utility and heavy transport jobs. Here's a tandem rear axle mixer with pusher and tag axles. Options were 210 to 450 horsepower motors and 9- or 10-speed manual or five-speed automatic transmissions with 2- or 3-speed auxiliary gears. (OTC)

For work as an on/off highway transporter, Oshkosh built the 1978 R Series tandem rear axle truck. The engine range for these monsters was 280 to 360 horsepower. Transmission choices included 9- to 13-speed manual gear boxes with two-speed auxiliary transmissions available on some models. (OTC)

In 1978, sales of White trucks hit 14,598 ranking the company sixth in Class 7/Class 8 deliveries. The big news was that White was talking with M.A.N. of Germany about selling a 50 percent stake in the Eastlake, Ohio truck maker. This is the Road Boss 2 model hooked to a Fruehauf trailer. (WTC)

Big trucks shone in a clouded 1979 auto market realizing a two percent gain over 1978. FWD built 389 heavy-duty Class 8 diesels and specialized Seagraves at its Clintonville, Wisconsin plant, up from 353 in 1978. This Tractioneer dump truck was equipped for snow removal work. (FWD)

A 1979 FWD 8 x 8 cement mixer chassis. The Wisconsin builder of heavy-duty trucks was benefiting greatly from the boom in mining and construction in the United States at this time. This led to the creation of new models like a BXM wheel tractor and front discharge cement mixer chassis. (FWD)

Conventional models in the 1979 FWD range included this all-wheel drive cab and chassis with a 4 x 4 configuration. The company was seeing its highest production since 1975, when 472 trucks had been assembled. Bertrand A. McKittrick was chairman; Ernest W. Karlenzig was president and COE. (FWD)

A 1979 Chevrolet C70 highway tractor. Chevrolet's 1979 registrations by GVW included 445,549 trucks of 6,000 pounds or less; 591,506 of 6,001 to 10,000 pounds; 4,948 of 10,001 to 14,000 pounds; 1,786 of 16,001 to 19,500 pounds; 34,892 of 19,501 to 26,000 pounds; 1,139 of 26,001 to 33,000 pounds; and 5,050 over 33,001 pounds. (CMD)

A downturn in the overall heavy-duty truck market in the last half of 1979 spelled doomsday for Chevrolets like this Titan SS, as the announcement came down from GM brass that all Class 7 and Class 8 sales would be consolidated under the GMC banner effective in October 1980. (CMD)

Chevrolet's tough new 1979 linehauler was nicknamed the "Poppa Bear" Bruin. It offered five series of diesel engines for quick response to power demands. Design-wise, the Bruin offered 90-1/2-inch top corner cab clearance permitting room for most 45-foot long trailer operations. (CMD)

116" BBC Chevy Bison.

Chevrolet's ability to market trucks like this 1979 Bison 116-inch BBC tractor was limited by the fact that only 150 dealers offered them. As a result, only 3,674 "heavy Chevys" were sold that calendar year. Bisons had the power to pull large tanker-trailers over the American highways. (CMD)

In 1979, International Harvester Company kept the lead in heavy-duty American truck sales. The total of 70,903 retail deliveries for the calendar year was a 31.3 percent increase over 1978's numbers. This 1979 Transtar 4300 conventional highway tractor was among the company's 75-odd models. (IHC)

Another model available from Allentown, Pennsylvania's best-known truck company in 1979 was the Mack Super-Liner. During the year, Mack built a prototype truck for United Parcel Service which met the new federal 75 decibels Class A noise level regulations. (MTC)

Mack's Value-Liner was another important part of the company's 1979 model line. Early in 1979, the company said it would begin to phase out its unprofitable off-highway vehicle production. Later, it announced plans to invest $30 million to design a new series for release in the mid-1980s. (MTC)

Oshkosh's B Series forward placement mixer came with driving or non-driving front axles. A tandem rear axle was standard, with pusher or tag axle options. It had a 210 to 290 horsepower engine range with 6- to 10-speed manual gear boxes or 4- and 5-speed automatics, plus a two-speed transfer case. (OTC)

The 1979 Western Star was a custom-built Class 8 cab-over with sleeper introduced by White Motor Corporation in 1978. White's corporate offices moved from suburban Cleveland to Farmington Hills, Michigan in 1979. The firm's Exton, Pennsylvania factory was closed and Autocar production moved to Ogden, Utah.

The big truck market was uneven in 1980 and GMC dealers retailed 42,805 medium- and heavy-duty trucks. That was a 17 percent decline from 1979, but still enough to make GMC tops in Class 7 and Class 8 sales. This GMC General was among 18,700 Class 7 and Class 8 trucks built that year. (GMC)

GMC's 1980 Brigadier heavy-duty short conventional truck featured new air-brake plumbing designed for quick access and easier serviceability. Also new was a standard bumper with flexible end caps bolted to a steel center section. On impact, the ends deflected and returned to their original shape. (GMC)

Mack retailed 21,991 big Class 8 diesel trucks for 1980, when this Cruise-Liner COE sleeper cab was sold. That made the Allentown, Pennsylvania company America's number two maker of such models, second to International-Harvester, but only by three percent. Mack began exploring the transit bus market. (MTC)

Mack Truck chairman Alfred W. Pelletier laid blame for declining sales of trucks like this 1980 Cruise-Liner on a weak United States economy, especially in the automotive and construction industries. This cut the demand for over-the-road transportation of goods. (MTC)

Another model offered by Mack in 1980 was the Super-Liner diesel conventional. This one, with its twin-plated chromed exhausts, is hooked to a Fruehauf trailer. This publicity photo certainly projects the image of the long-distance truck driver as the "last American cowboy." (MTC)

Perfectly at home with large, heavy hauling jobs was the 1980 Mack Super-Liner. However, the firm's new product was the Mack Mid-Liner Class 6 diesel, built in France and imported into the United States through a Mack/Regie Renault deal. Its sales were 800 in the United States and 700 in Canada. (MTC)

All of Mack's 1980 shipments from United States plants involved trucks in the 33,001 pounds and over heavy-duty GVW class, such as this Cruise-Liner at work on a dock in San Francisco, California. The shipments totaled 24,618 units. In 1980, Mack predicted a slow and gradual sales recovery. (MTC)

White Motor Corporation entered a Chapter 11 reorganization in September, 1980. One of the company's products was the Western Star line, which offered a wide range of models including this conventional sleeper cab diesel hooked to a long Trailmobile trailer. (WTC)

A new 1981 Ford F-800 conventional cab truck with an Omaha Standard livestock body. Ford shipped 617,326 trucks this year, including 142,004 of 6,000 pounds or less; 414,310 of 6,001 to 10,000 pounds; 18,035 of 19,501 to 26,000 pounds; 29,339 of 26,001 to 33,000 pounds and 13,638 of more than 33,000 pounds. (FMC)

GMC supplied the "Official Truck" for the 65th running of the Indianapolis 500-Mile Race on May 26, 1981. As part of the promotion, this GMC 3/4-ton with a Holmes wrecker body was supplied to the Indianapolis Motor Speedway Corporation for use during the race. (IMSC)

The 1982 GMC General was available with an optional "Five Star" interior and exterior trim package. Standard features included the soft ride cab mounting with adjustable air springs and shocks at the rear of the cab. A control valve allowed drivers to adjust the air pressure for maximum ride comfort. (GMC)

The 1982 GMC Series 8000 Brigadier came only with diesel power. A new turbo version of the Caterpillar 3208 engine was offered in the heavy-duty Series 9500 Brigadier, which also had new transmissions and improved axles available for all models. In 1982, GMC retailed 28,522 Class 5 to Class 8 models. (GMC)

A 1982 GMC medium-duty grain-box body truck. GMC shipped 227,618 trucks that year, including 107,444 of 6,000 pounds or less; 83,372 6,001 to 10,000 pounds; 1,107 of 16,001 to 19,500 pounds; 7,760 of 19,501 to 26,500 pounds; 14,204 of 26,001 to 33,000 pounds and 8,731 of more than 33,000 pounds. (GMC)

A 1982 GMC "Top Kick" medium-duty was used for this sturdy dump truck. One drawback to 1982 sales was deregulation of the trucking industry. It put small freight carriers out of business and loaded the marketplace with a surplus of used trucks. GMC had 15.5 percent of the medium- and heavy-duty truck market.

Still turning out a few hundred trucks a year in Clintonville, Wisconsin was the FWD Company. This is the firm's 1983 COE truck cab. A total of 1,165 non-mainstream specialty trucks shipments were made that calendar year in the United States. Of these, 631 were Class 7 models and 409 were Class 8s. (FWD)

A 1983 GMC General heavy-duty with tank trailer. GMC shipped 263,773 trucks that year, including 138,364 of 6,000 pounds or less; 93,771 of 6,001 to 10,000 pounds; 960 of 16,001 to 19,500 pounds; 8,931 of 19,501 to 26,500 pounds; 12,014 of 26,001 to 33,000 pounds and 9,733 of more than 33,000 pounds. (GMC)

In 1983, GMC offered hydraulic disc brakes as standard equipment on certain medium-duty truck models, such as this 6000 Series dump truck. The new brake system was a 50/50 split design featuring separate hydraulic brake lines between the front and rear axles. (GMC)

Expanded engine offerings, new tandem rear axles and five-speed transmissions were available for GMC medium-duty trucks for 1983. The axles had a wide range of economy and performance ratios to suit a variety of applications. The new transmission was suited for mid-range diesels and large gas engines. (GMC)

General Motors marketed a new-for-1984 low cab forward (LCF) truck under Chevrolet Tiltmaster and GMC Forward nameplates, the latter seen here with diesel power. This tilt-cab truck was built by Isuzu Motors Limited of Japan. It contributed 1,700 deliveries to GMC's medium-duty sales picture. (GMC)

A factory-installed work body available for Dodge Ram trucks was the Road Ready Stake Truck. Dodge's total factory shipments for the 1984 calendar year included 145,667 trucks with GVWs under 6,000 pounds and 69,971 in the 6,001 to 10,000 pound weight class. (DTD)

GMC had a big year selling big Class 8s like this General in 1984. Many truck fleets were replacing old equipment or expanding to meet new business demands. Sales leaped to 14,282 from just 7,443 last season, a 92 percent increase. New was a standard Bostram low-back air suspension driver's seat. (GMC)

Though building only light-duty 1985 trucks in two classes, Dodge offered "Road Ready" factory-installed work bodies for chassis-and-cab models with heavy-duty extras. Included was this 1-1/2 yard dump truck based on the Dodge Ram in the 6,0001 to 10,000 pound GVW class with dual rear wheels. (DTD)

Mack's 1983 sales included 12,549 Class 8 trucks like this Model MH Ultra-Liner COE tractor. Playing a larger role in the firm's business were Renault-built Class 6 and Class 7 Mack Mid-Liner models with respective sales of 2,428 and 1,059 units. Renault's share in Mack went from 20 to 50 percent in 1983. (MTC)

The 12-foot 1985 Dodge Kary Van II was another Road Ready model-option featuring a heavy-type truck body for what was actually a light-duty model. This greatly expanded the make's appeal to buyers who wanted to purchase sturdy work trucks at an affordable price. (DTD)

On October 29, 1986, Mack Trucks delivered the 25,000th Renault-built Mid-Liner sold by the company since entering the Class 6 and Class 7 medium-duty market in 1980. The truck was delivered to Capitol Foods, Incorporated of Atlanta, Georgia which had 86 trucks, more than half of them Macks. (MTC)

Another Road Ready truck was the 1985 Model 528 Dodge Ram "Retriever" tow truck. This factory-optional package was available for the standard-size pickup with dual rear wheels and heavy-duty suspension. (DTD)

Posing with a 1988 GMC medium-duty truck that hauled his piano to work is Eugene Istomin, the world-renowned concert pianist. The specially-equipped Top Kick cargo van accompanied the musician on his 1988-1989 North American Tour organized by Shaw Concerts. (GMC)

A moving man (left) wearing a Washington Redskins shirt helps load Eugene Istomin's grand piano on the 1988 GMC truck built for his tour. The company's Class 4 to Class 8 production fell to 33,175 units when a January, 1988 joint venture with Volvo took GMC out of heavy-duty truck production. (GMC)

This early 1988 GMC Hot Shot truck was specially equipped by Nalley Motor Trucks of Atlanta, Georgia and Fontaine Truck Modification Center of Pontiac, Michigan with an aerodynamic 60-inch Able Body stand-up sleeper, a low-mount fifth wheel, stainless quarter fenders and deck plate, a vacuum trailer brake system, swivel captain chairs and a front air dam with driving lights. (GMC)

A great 1988 work truck was the GMC Value Van 35. This 1-ton cab-forward model came with both steel and aluminum bodies and in a variety of body lengths suitable for many job applications. GMC was preparing to relocate all of its medium-duty truck production to Janesville, Wisconsin for 1989. (GMC)

The 1988 Magnavan from GMC truck. In the 1988 calendar year, GMC shipped 231,592 trucks with GVWs under 6,000 pounds; 120,222 of 6,001 to 10,000 pounds; 5,371 of 16,001 to 19,500 pounds; 13,408 of 19,501 to 26,000 pounds; 16,421 of 26,001 to 33,000 pounds and 733 of over 33,000 pounds. (GMC)

Again in 1988, GMC supplied "Official Trucks" for the Indy 500. For race-day emergencies, the company also provided this "GMC Motorsports" trimmed 1-ton chassis and cab with dual rear wheels and a medium-duty Challenger wrecker body. The 72nd Indy 500 was held on May 29, 1988. (GMC)

Chevrolet's C6 medium had a LoPro option package and 14,840 to 16,000 pound GVWs. In calendar year 1989, Chevrolet shipped 883,478 trucks with GVWs under 6,000 pounds; 320,109 of 6,001 to 10,000 pounds; 94 of 16,001 to 19,500 pounds; 7,341 of 19,501 to 26,000 pounds; and 7,981 of over 33,000 pounds. (CMD)

Chevrolet sold 15,930 medium- and heavy-duty trucks in 1989. They included 234 Class 5s, 7,424 Class 6s and 8,272 Class 7s. The 1989 Chevrolet Kodiak C70 conventional cab came with a variety of engine and transmission options for heavy-duty hauling work. (CMD)

Offered again in 1989 was the Isuzu-made Chevrolet Tiltmaster. The W7 (Class 7) version is pictured here at work in a lumberyard setting. It has a Turbo Diesel power plant and a handy platform body with a rack-type front end. (CMD)

Loaded with hay is a 1989 Chevrolet medium-duty truck with a platform and stake rack body shown at work on the farm. This was the first year in recent automotive history that Chevrolet posted no heavy-duty truck sales due to the merger of GM's Class 8 operations with Volvo-White Truck Corporation. (CMD)

A new 1989 GMC GMT350 stake truck. In the 1989 calendar year, GMC shipped 237,480 trucks with GVWs under 6,000 pounds; 111,063 of 6,001 to 10,000 pounds; 4,462 of 16,001 to 19,500 pounds; 6,661 of 19,501 to 26,000 pounds; 13,631 of 26,001 to 33,000 pounds and 98 of over 33,000 pounds. (GMC)

Featuring a big International conventional chassis, this 1989 tanker was under construction at Pierce Manufacturing, in Appleton, Wisconsin, the world's largest producer of fire fighting apparatus. It was being built for the Brookfield, Connecticut Fire Department. (OCW)

The Georgetown Fire Department ordered this 1989 Pierce cab-over-engine Tilt-Cab pumper. It was one of 3,571 big trucks constructed in the United States by "miscellaneous" manufacturers in calendar year 1989. Of these, the bulk of 2,039 were Class 8s.

The 1988 merger of GMC's Class 8 operations with Volvo-White led to Volvo GM Heavy Truck Corporation and reduced sales of heavy-duty GMCs. Emphasis switched to smaller models like this 1990 GMC Top-Kick delivery van. (GMC)

This 1990 GMC model P-3500 commercial cab and chassis could be ordered with GVW ratings up to 14,100 pounds. This example is fitted with a high-cube van body. The P-model was also used for 80 to 90 percent of all motorhomes. (GMC)

Hard at work is a 1990 Autocar model ACM 31-yard rear packer refuse truck. This model gave unsurpassed performance when a premium, custom-built truck was required. It offered maximum maneuverability, visibility and strength. (WGM)

In 1991, Chevrolet launched its new C/K3500 Heavy-Duty 1-Ton-Plus line of trucks. The C3500s were 4 x 2 conventionals, while K3500s (such as this one with a special utility-dump body) were equipped with four-wheel drive. (CMD)

The 1991 Chevrolet C3500HD commercial cab and chassis made the perfect base for a tilt-bed tow truck. This one, used by Classic Restorations, had no problem carrying a restored 1959 Chevrolet El Camino pickup. (CMD)

"Driven with pride" was the slogan used to promote sales of this 1991 WhiteGMC tall integral sleeper cab. It featured an 8-foot 6-inch high sleeping compartment with 22 cubic feet of stand-up room behind the seats. (WGM)

The launch of a new Crew Cab pickup took center stage in Chevrolet's 1992 truck line. It was offered in C3500 two-wheel drive and K3500 four-wheel drive configurations and had a longer wheelbase and more rear seat legroom. (CMD)

Volvo GM Heavy Truck's 1992 WIA was a new model designed to save operators $1,400 over previous WCMs and $3,500 over other high-hood conventionals. It featured a 15-degree tapered hood for a six percent wind drag reduction. (WGM)

WhiteGMC Volvo began making its 1992 FE model in the United States. FEs were well-suited for fighting inter-city traffic for local distribution. They could jog around perimeters and cross-county in daily intra-city service, too. (WGM)

The 1992 Volvo FE LCOE (low cab-over-engine) truck was built to survive years of rigorous duty with minimum downtime. This one has a tractor with a Thermo-King refrigeration unit for delivery of fresh flowers to retailers. (WGM)

WhiteGMC Xpeditor trucks are made with high-efficiency heavy hauling in mind. This 1992 model has a Leach refuse truck body. Xpeditors are available with 84-inch or 95-1/2-inch wide precision-welded, galvanized steel cabs. (WGM)

The flexibility of the 1992 WhiteGMC Xpeditor chassis permitted many unique applications for these trucks. This one was built for Ogden Aviation Services as a multi-compartment tanker to fuel jet aircraft. (WGM)

The 1993 International 9300 conventional tractor is seen here with top-of-the-line Eagle trim. This is the most spacious flat-sided riveted aluminum cab on the road today. It measures 76-inches wide and up to 60-inches high. (IHC)

International's 9200/9400 series trucks are available with new chassis aero skirting and a choice of a chrome wraparound aluminum bumper or a black, color-impregnated aero bumper. This 1993 also has the Eagle package. (IHC)

The 1993 International 9600 Aero offers a choice of spacious sleepers including a 110-inch Hi-Rise model, the flat-roof Pro-Sleeper and 89- or 110-inch flat-roof models. The aerodynamic roof fairing has side extenders. (IHC)

Design features in the 1993 International 9600 include its set-forward axle, a reliable and durable cab-over-engine configuration and aerodynamic enhancements to reduce wind resistance and up fuel economy. (IHC)

The International 4000 Series fire truck chassis features the only factory-installed four-door Travelcrew cab in the industry. The 4000s come with a range of diesel engines including a heavy-duty power plant with 300 horsepower. (IHC)

With its lightweight componentry, tanker operations are a natural for the 1993 International 9200 Class 8 tractor. It is available with Cummins or Caterpillar engines with 280 to 350 horsepower. (IHC)

International 2000 series trucks are built for rugged on/off highway use. For 1993, the 2000s are offered as 2500 models with a set-forward front axle or 2600s with a set-back front axle. This dump truck is a 2500. (IHC)

The sure-footed WhiteGMC Xpeditor series returned for 1993 with its easy-to-maneuver low cab forward design. Dependable Sanitation Company of New York uses this truck with a Leach refuse vehicle body mounted. (WGM)

Reflecting the continuation of consolidations and mergers in the truck-building industry, this is a 1993 Autocar truck manufactured by the WhiteGMC branch of Volvo GM Heavy Truck Corporation. Autocars promised "all muscle, no fat" with power plant options up to a 460-horsepower diesel. (WGM)

An unusual photograph in a 1993 WhiteGMC Volvo sales catalog for WG series trucks pictured what is described as an "axle-pounding, gut-busting, down-in-the-mud" tri-axle chassis and cab with a Twin-States dump truck body. (WGM)

299

Hard at work protecting the environment is a 1994 International 4000 series model 4900 twin-axle truck with a trash compactor body. With the "greening" of America, trucks of this type are finding a growing market today. (IHC)

A 1994 International Paystar 5000 series truck makes a good base for a large cement mixer. A product of Navistar International Transportation Corporation, International trucks are available today at 900 dealers nationwide. (IHC)

International's 2000 series trucks are well-suited for a variety of purpose-built bodies designed for special applications in industry. This 2600 model was designed for service as a tri-axle utility vehicle. (IHC)

Featuring the upscale Eagle interior trim package, this 1994 International 9300 conventional semi-tractor rolls down the American highway with a tandem tanker-trailer system in tow. (IHC)

Designed for fleet use, the 1994 WhiteGMC integral sleeper aero features a set-back axle designed to optimize weight distribution and improve handling. The exclusive one-piece cabin adds space and reduces noise. (WGM)

WhiteGMC's 1994 ACL Autocar conventional combines quality and durability in a slope-hood style tractor. It is available in axle-forward or axle-back options and combines lightweight construction with heavy-duty components. (WGM)

303